CUSTOMER SENSE

CUSTOMER SENSE

How the 5 Senses Influence
Buying Behavior

ARADHNA KRISHNA

palgrave
macmillan

CUSTOMER SENSE

First published in 2013 by
PALGRAVE MACMILLAN®
in the United States—a division of St. Martin's Press LLC,
175 Fifth Avenue, New York, NY 10010.

Where this book is distributed in the UK, Europe and the rest of the world,
this is by Palgrave Macmillan, a division of Macmillan Publishers Limited,
registered in England, company number 785998, of Houndmills,
Basingstoke, Hampshire RG21 6XS.

Palgrave Macmillan is the global academic imprint of the above companies
and has companies and representatives throughout the world.

Palgrave® and Macmillan® are registered trademarks in the United States,
the United Kingdom, Europe and other countries.

ISBN: 978–0–230–34173–9

Library of Congress Cataloging-in-Publication Data

Krishna, Aradhna.
    Customer sense : how the 5 senses influence buying behavior /
Aradhna Krishna.
        p. cm.
    ISBN 978–0–230–34173–9 (alk. paper)
        1. Marketing—Psychological aspects. 2. Consumer behavior. 3. Senses
and sensation. I. Title.

HF5415.K674 2013
658.8′342—dc23   2012035568

A catalogue record of the book is available from the British Library.

Design by Newgen Imaging Systems (P) Ltd., Chennai, India.

First edition: April 2013

10 9 8 7 6 5 4 3 2 1

Printed in Hong Kong.

To Papa for introducing me to sensorially lush things in life—chocolate, crisp toast, corduroy, Himalayan air, horse manure, and shoe polish…
and to Ma, Vidya, and Meera

CONTENTS

CONTENTS

ILLUSTRATIONS

ACKNOWLEDGMENTS

I WAS WALKING BACK FROM COLUMBIA Health Services to my office in Uris Hall in 1990 when I realized that I always took one of two possible paths. I wondered why. As any curious academic would, I drew the map on a piece of paper and went down the hall asking my colleagues which of the two paths they would choose. I was intrigued when nearly all chose one path over the other. Next was the question of why? Why did they choose one of two equidistant paths from point A to point B? My research into sensory marketing and more specifically visual perception was born at that time. I later came up with the new Direct Distance bias whereby shorter direct distances between endpoints of two non-straight paths make the paths appear shorter.

Since then, over two decades I have conducted hundreds of studies on issues of sensory perception. As such, this book has taken me more than twenty years to write. The book integrates my research as well as that of others in marketing, cognitive psychology, and neuroscience with a view to how it can be applied in the real world. As such, it is full of real life examples and borrows heavily from courses on sensory marketing that I have developed and teach to BBAs, MBAs, and also to middle- and senior-level executives.

Given the long-time effort to put this book together, I am indebted to numerous people. First, I would like to thank Kurtis Droge-Germain who did a remarkable job in helping me with the actual writing of my material sometimes even adding new examples on his own. The book would have been delayed by at least another year without his help. Much of the research discussed in this book was conducted with colleagues (Mimi Morrin, Priya Raghubir, and Norbert Schwarz), my doctoral students (Nilufer Aydinoglu, Ryan Elder, Eda Sayin), and my post-doc (Luca Cian). I owe them many thanks for all the conversations we had that have honed my thinking over the years and made the research fun. Ryan Elder, in particular, has been a major stalwart in my efforts to grow this field. Contributors to the Sensory Marketing Conference, especially Joan Meyers-Levy, Joann Peck, and Laura Peracchio, were incredibly helpful in structuring hundreds of published papers into a graspable form.

I would also like to thank multiple research and teaching assistants I have had since 2009 who helped me pull together examples for the book—Jennifer Song, Aexa Barron, Ted Herringshaw, Stacey Shuman, Katherine Cohen, Gabriel Bilen, Freya Rajeshwar, Nisha Sheth, Eileen Jen. Ashley Clise, and Cara Herman. The Ross School of Business and the University of Michigan have supported me in my endeavors and provided me with the resources I need.

Many new ideas were discussed with my friends Norbert Schwarz, Daphna Oyserman, David Wooten, Poonam Arora, Matt Hull, and Kriszti Fehervary over chai or wine. Andy, Harish, Arvind, Sonia, Manish, Swati, Namita, Poonam, Seema, Sunita, Yan, Marjorie, Gayatri, and Ruma energized me. Jag, Sidd, and Kamya let me talk to them about research I was excited about at that instant. Their incisive and often caustic comments made me think much harder about sensation and perception and its role in marketing.

Chapter 1

INTRODUCTION: WHAT IS
SENSORY MARKETING?

LIBRARIES AND ICE CREAM

In 1990 the Ross School of Business in Ann Arbor faced a miniature crisis. After the library announced that many journals and books would be available only in electronic form, the faculty rose up in protest. When asked to explain their reasoning in opposing the switch, faculty members found it difficult to express their opinions. They came up with such responses as "I like to feel the paper," "I love the smell of libraries," or "It's just not the same thing!" They knew that such seemingly feeble reasons could not prevent the change to electronic media, so they tried to rephrase their sentiments in ways that would sound more logical and appropriate for professors in a business school. The responses they came up with included that the atmosphere was conducive to work and that the physical nature of the journals led them to peruse related articles in the same publication.

Similarly, the prevalence of online books and reading materials has changed the way students interact with their courses. Since many textbooks are available online for a reduced fee or even for free and since online texts are available wherever there is Internet access, it would seem that almost all students would jump at the opportunity and ditch paper books for good. However, this has not been the case. While some students try to use online materials whenever possible, a good number still order physical textbooks, course packs, and other books for their classes. When asked why, students come up with the same types of responses as the faculty at the Ross School of Business and cite the feel of the book, the smell of the paper, or the ability to "cozy up with a book." When they realize how absurd their reasons sound, students turn to rationalizations, claiming that text is harder to read on the computer screen or that some online texts are not amenable to note taking and bookmarking.

These stories would seem to suggest that there is something more to a book or a library than just a collection of printed pages or a collection of books. That something is hard to define, and although people are embarrassed to admit to its existence when they are affected by it, it is certainly real. Furthermore, it is not illogical; there is nothing stupid, old-fashioned, or irrational in saying that the feel of a book is worth shelling out a few dollars more for than for simply owning an online copy. This phenomenon is very relevant to products like the Kindle and the Nook, recent introductions by Amazon and Barnes & Noble that serve as electronic book readers. While they are convenient and innovative, if the previously mentioned stories are at all reflective of the views of the general public, they will have trouble entirely eclipsing paper books.

While the Ross faculty was protesting the removal of paper library materials, Curt Jones, a recent university graduate and prospective entrepreneur, was working on developing a company to manufacture his extraordinary invention. What was his new product idea? It consisted of taking modified ice cream mix and flash freezing it in liquid nitrogen (don't try this one at home). The resulting product tasted like ice cream, only it was more concentrated and shaped like small blobs or dots, rather than being smooth in texture. He called the substance Dippin' Dots. His marketing strategy was to brand Dippin' Dots as the "Ice Cream of the Future" and to focus on selling it through stands in amusement parks, carnivals, and other venues rather than through more conventional channels of food sales such as supermarkets. The product was wildly successful. The company had over 27 million dollars in revenue in 2011, having enjoyed over 15 years of steady profits. But just what is it that makes consumers willing to pay $2 more for Dippin' Dots than for regular ice cream?

It isn't about taste. Dippin' Dots comes in the same types of flavors as normal ice cream, and its taste is remarkably similar to that of ice cream. However, the experience of eating Dippin' Dots could not be more different from that of eating an ice cream cone. The texture of the dots completely changes the way the product is consumed; instead of people licking or biting the ice cream, the beads melt and burst in the consumer's mouth. While the product might seem to be very similar to ice cream, just as physical and electronic books might seem to be very similar at first glance, the two are actually very different, and not for a silly or illogical reason.

What the irate Ross faculty and the ice-cream-loving little children tell us is that there can be more to a product than meets the eye. In fact, there can be more to a product than meets the ear, nose, mouth, or fingers as well. Many attributes of products are based on interactions between the senses or on senses consumers may not even be aware of. There is a science to studying these attributes, the senses that perceive them, the psychology that drives those senses, and the ways products can appeal to and make use of peoples' senses. Based on that science, I have defined *sensory marketing* as "marketing that engages the consumers' senses and affects their perception, judgment, and behavior."[1]

SENSORY SIGNATURES IN ACTION

Many products have very recognizable attributes that appeal to one or more of the senses. As an example, try the following exercise. Close your eyes for about ten seconds and imagine the color pink. What do you think of? Now try again, except this time imagine a ribbon as well. What do you think of the second time around? Most people in the second case would think of the movement to fight breast cancer, and a fair number of people in the first case would think of that movement as well. However, this is not due to mere chance.

The pink ribbon was developed as the logo for Susan G. Komen for the Cure, which is the largest organization in the United States dedicated to fighting breast cancer. While the pink ribbon, much like the golden arches of McDonald's, is a logo, it is also more than that. The color pink alone causes many people to think about the breast cancer movement and now adorns everything from yogurt containers to subway cars in support of that movement. This indicates that the pink ribbon has transcended the realm of the logo. It has become what I have deemed a *sensory signature*. One way to think about a sensory signature is as a concept, often a brand name, that is evoked by a combination of sensations, much like the breast cancer movement is called to mind by the color pink.

Another way to think about sensory signatures is as the combination of sensations evoked by a concept, often a brand name. Consider the Microsoft Corporation, and, more specifically, the Windows operating system. What comes to mind? Some people will picture the four-colored logo that appears when computers with Windows boot up. Other people will imagine the sound that accompanies that logo. There is no right or wrong answer as to the question of which of those two sensations is the one that is more closely or immediately associated with Microsoft; some people may even have imagined both. Interestingly enough, people with an East Asian cultural background tend to picture the logo with greater frequency than people with a Western cultural background; this is possibly due to the fact that many Asian scripts are pictorial.[2] Either way, both the logo and the sound are part of Microsoft's sensory signature.

Figure 1.1 Microsoft Logo.
When you think of Microsoft, do you think of the visual logo above, or do you think of a particular sound?

As with Microsoft, a sensory signature can encompass elements pertaining to many senses. This is the case with 5 Gum, a brand of chewing gum that claims to be able to "stimulate your senses." Its brand name is built on the idea of having a sensory signature that appeals to all five senses. This contrasts with the traditional view of chewing gum mainly appealing to taste, with the other senses being limited to perhaps a brightly colored box design or the Wrigley's advertising jingle. In contrast, 5 Gum also tries to get consumers to focus on what it feels like to chew the gum, emphasizing that there is more to the product than just taste.

Sensory signatures can also focus on a specific sense that one would not normally associate with the product in question. One example of this is Axe's Dark Temptation advertisement, which features a man covered in chocolate surrounded by several attractive females. While one might normally associate a scent with a certain deodorant, the Dark Temptation advertisement focuses on touch and taste rather than smell. In addition, it connects the product with sexual desire, much like many other deodorant advertisements, in order to create a specific feeling about the product.

Other types of sensory signatures simply try to highlight a particular sensation that consumers already associate with the product. The iPod Touch, for example, connects the sensation of touch with a music player to show that the product has aspects that appeal to touch in addition to hearing. Not only does the name of the product convey the sense of touch, but the design of the touch screen fits in with consumers' expectations once they hear the name. The product is meant to be touched, pressed, played with, spun, and used with the fingers.

A BRIEF HISTORY OF SENSORY MARKETING

The concept of sensory marketing is not new. If we could ask a person from ancient times who lived in the Mediterranean world what came to his mind when he imagined the color purple, he would probably have named the city of Tyre. A metropolis in Phoenicia (today's Lebanon), the city of Tyre became famous for Tyrian purple, a distinctive color of dye that was extracted by its citizens from sea snails. Because the color, which became known (or branded, if we look at it from the marketer's perspective) as royal or imperial purple, was so unique, the city was able to establish a virtual monopoly of the dye for many years, generating great wealth and prosperity.

Turning to more recent times, I have divided the evolution of marketing in the post-World War II era into three phases.[3] The first phase, sometimes known as the no-nonsense era, came immediately after the war in the 1950s and 1960s. Consumers were focused on practical aspects of goods, emphasizing their utility and cost. The second phase, generally held to have begun in the 1970s, saw a massive increase in branding. Companies began to realize that a brand name, such as Levi's, could have value in and of itself. Hand in hand with the rise of brand names came an increase in advertising expenditures as companies tried to build their own or attack their competitors' brands. The third phase is the modern era, which has been marked by the rise of the Internet and the increasing awareness of companies of the sensory attributes of products.

Though many companies are only now becoming aware of the existence of sensory attributes, that does not mean that they did not unknowingly manipulate them in the past. The key difference between then and now is in the awareness, not in the execution. One classic example of a sensory signature is Tiffany Blue, the shade of light blue that can be found in many of the products made by Tiffany & Co., the New York jewelry company. Though Tiffany Blue is not usually the primary color in the company's products, it is almost always present in some form, whether as an accent, a background, or an element interwoven in the design. While Tiffany Blue was certainly not developed with sensory marketing in mind, it has proven to be one of the most prevalent and recognizable sensory signatures to date. Another example of this phenomenon is the lemon scent that has been added to many brands of dishwashing detergent. Many years ago, companies found that consumers had a more favorable reaction to a fruity smell than to just a soapy one, so they added lemon scent to their products, and it caught on.

Nowadays, companies are finding and developing exciting new products with unique and attractive sensory attributes. One particularly strange and exotic product that has come on the market is the fish pedicure service that has been popping up around the globe. In a service similar to a spa treatment, consumers pay in order to submerge their feet into a pond or a tub teeming with so-called doctor fish or *Garra rufa*. These fish are said to have therapeutic properties, eating away dead skin so that new, healthy skin can grow. While the sensation is very strange at first—and the thought of thousands of tiny fish nibbling away at one's feet is eerie, to say the least—most people who try it find the experience soothing and rejuvenating after they get over their initial apprehensions.

Another leading trend in creating new sensations can be found in the restaurant industry. El Bulli, a restaurant in Catalonia, Spain, has been a pioneer in the field of molecular gastronomy, sometimes also known as culinary physics. A recently developed discipline, culinary physics seeks to use various techniques from chemistry and the other sciences to manipulate the texture, feel, smell, or shape of food. With dinners costing as much as 250 euros a plate, meals cooked using molecular gastronomy are clearly very sought after, but it's not only a matter of taste. Having access to experiences such as eating partially solidified bubbles of juice or eggs cooked at the perfect temperature to affect their shape is worth something to consumers, indicating that molecular gastronomy is a field that transcends the sense of taste to create a complete sensory experience. Another line of restaurants, whose US brand is named Opaque, seeks to stimulate the other four senses by treating consumers to "Dining in the Dark." Opaque focuses on tastes, smells, sounds, and the feel of the food by crafting a very specific, dark, environment. These new types of sensory experiences suggest that companies and marketers are just starting to catch on to the importance of the different sensory attributes of their products and services.

SENSATION AND PERCEPTION

The Irish idealist philosopher George Berkeley, who lived in the first half of the eighteenth century, famously said that "To be is to be perceived."[4] Though the exact meaning of this quote has been debated by philosophers studying his work ever since, one thing is certain: Berkeley stumbled upon a key insight when he linked the notion of being (or sensation, in other words) to the notion of perception. While one could argue that, philosophically speaking, the two are the same—that is, that the tree falling in the forest when no one can hear it does not make a sound—scientifically speaking, the two concepts are quite distinct.

One of Berkeley's earliest works, a treatise entitled *An Essay Towards a New Theory of Vision*, includes a discussion of what became known as Molyneux's problem, after the Frenchman William Molyneux. Molyneux questioned whether a man who was blind his whole life would be able to distinguish between a sphere and a cube solely by looking at them were he to suddenly regain his sight. What both Berkeley and his frequent opponent John Locke agreed upon was that the blind man would not be able to tell the difference. Despite having touched spheres and cubes many times, the man would not be able to associate the visual contours of the two objects with the sensations of touch that he had experienced. While the answer to Molyneux's problem is understandably difficult to test in an experiment, what Berkeley and Locke's reasoning tells us is that the mere appearance of the sphere and the cube could very well be meaningless unless we are able to interpret those appearances mentally and process their meaning.

Hence arose the distinction between sensation and perception. Information, when taken in from any of our senses, travels to the thalamus, which is a central station in the brain. The thalamus is named based on the Greek word for "brain," which also carries the connotation of a couch on which the two halves of the brain rest. When the information reaches the thalamus, a sensation is produced. This sensation is simply the registration of a sound or of rays of light. The thalamus then passes a signal on to the cortex, which is a wrinkled mass of nerve cells that surrounds both halves of the brain. When the information reaches the cortex, it is interpreted as a certain sound or a certain shape, and this is called a perception.

One easy way to illustrate the difference between sensation and perception is through optical illusions, such as the two reprinted below. The one on the left, known as the Ponzo illusion, asks the viewer which girl appears larger. Most people, at least at first glance, would answer that the girl on the right appears bigger. In fact, the three girls are the same size. While the sensations of the rays of light that bounce off the three girls are identical, the mind's perception of the meaning of those signals is not, causing the difference in perception even when the sensations are identical. Likewise with the drawing on the right: which line is longer? As an astute observer might have guessed, the two lines are of the same length. Even knowing this, though, it's hard not to "see" the line with the arrows facing outward as longer than the line with the arrows facing inward. As in the Ponzo illusion, though the sensations of the lines are the same, the mind's perceptions are quite different.

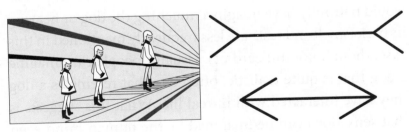

Figure 1.2 Optical Illusions (Ponzo and Two Lines with Arrows). Try out these optical illusions. Which girl looks larger? Which line looks longer?

One group of thinkers who explored the difference between sensation and perception was the Gestalt School, which flourished in Germany around the turn of the twentieth century. Known for distinguishing between what they termed "the whole" and "the parts," these thinkers accomplished pioneering work in developing optical illusions. They called one of their most notable discoveries the "phi phenomenon." In the phi phenomenon, the changing nature of a series of images produces the sensation of motion. Illustrated by a circle of dots wherein each dot briefly disappears and then reappears in sequence, the phi phenomenon is another example of how perceptions can be manipulated by carefully controlling sensations.

SENSORY IMAGERY

Take a moment to close your eyes and imagine interacting with a dog. It can be any type of dog; what is important is that you take around ten seconds or so to imagine interacting with the dog in your head. What experience came to mind? If you had to describe the dog, could you do so? Most people would describe visual characteristics of the dog, such as its color, size, age, or facial features. However, some people would naturally have imagined touching the dog or hearing its bark (smell and taste are less frequently mentioned in this case, though not unheard of). Usually, people can imagine a dog that is quite realistic, often one that resembles a dog they have interacted with in real life. What this suggests is that sensations can be imagined by the human mind even when they are not immediately at hand.

The fact that people can imagine sensations is called *sensory imagery*. Sensory imagery has many applications in the world around us. For example, an advertisement for a sweater in a magazine, while being a purely visual cue, could also cause us to imagine feeling the softness of the sweater.

Likewise, smelling a cookie could cause us to imagine tasting the cookie or feeling the texture of the chocolate chips in our mouth. Smelling the cookie could even cause us to imagine an experience from our childhood when we baked cookies in an Easy-Bake Oven. Sensory experiences are actually quite easy to imagine, if we put our minds to it.

One classic experiment in sensory imagery was conducted by C. W. Perky in 1910. A student of Edward Titchener, who was himself a student of Wilhelm Wundt, the so-called founder of experimental psychology, Perky wanted to investigate the boundaries between real sensations and sensory imagery. She asked people to imagine ordinary objects, such as a banana, a tomato, or a leaf while staring at a fixed point on a screen. Then, a color, very faint, but in the shape of the object that the subjects were trying to imagine, was projected onto the screen. The subjects did not even realize that they were witnessing a real sensory experience and merely attributed what they "saw" to their imagination.[5] Some participants seemed baffled when they tried to imagine a banana horizontally and instead imagined it vertically, but none of them suspected that the images existed anywhere outside of their own imagination. Perky's experiment suggests that the line between real sensations and sensory imagery may not be as clearly defined as we would imagine (for lack of a better word), and it has interesting applications for marketers attempting to use sensory imagery to advertise their products.

Not everyone is equally adept at imagining sensory experiences. How good do you think you are? Try thinking about the smell, taste, feel, sound, and sight of popcorn in a movie theater. How good are you at imagining each of these sensations?

An interesting exercise involving sensory imagery is to ask yourself what product you have the greatest sensory interaction with and what makes that interaction so special. Obviously, there is no right or wrong answer. Think about how vivid the experience is. When I ask my class about what their most vivid sensory interaction is, I am always surprised how different peoples' responses to their senses can be.

ABOUT THIS BOOK

I hope that so far I have been able to provide an overview of sensory marketing, some background about its development, and examples of products where it is used. From here, I will move on to talk about each sense in depth, including a description of how that sense works, examples of products and advertisements that have successfully used that sense in relation to sensory marketing, and researchers' past and present approaches to studying that sense.

The first chapter will discuss vision in greater detail. The notion of visual biases will be revisited, along with how marketers can make use of those biases. I will look at color to determine how color can influence consumer perceptions and influence the performance of tasks. Cultural preferences for certain colors will also be examined, with a focus on how different colors can be more or less effective in marketing depending on which area of the world the product is intended for. Finally, vision will be examined in the context of packaging, specifically the ways the design of a package can convey a variety of feelings with such simple changes as the placement of the photograph of the product on the package.

The next chapter discusses the sense of hearing. The nature of various sounds will be explored, as well as how the human body processes those sounds. The focus will again be on how those sounds can be used by marketers, answering such questions as what type of voice a spokesperson should have or what type of music a store should play depending on its target audience. The difference between types of sound patterns in languages will be connected to the concept of brand name design, again with an emphasis on how brand names are perceived by different cultures. In addition, the connections between hearing and the other senses will be explored.

The third chapter will discuss the sense of haptics or touch. The different types of touch, from incidental contact to consumers touching a product to figure out how it feels, will be examined. Touch will also be studied from the perspective of neuroscience, particularly in regard to how the science of the sense of touch can be applied to product design. Another approach to the concept of touch will be examined by considering what happens when two products touch or come into contact with each other. Finally, the concept of "need for touch," which encompasses people's different desires for haptic interaction at different levels, will be looked at.

The next section of the book will focus on smell. The connections between odors, emotions, and mood will be explored. How strong are the influences of smell on memory—can a specific scent really trigger a series of recollections? The implications of those connections for retailers and vendors will also be discussed. Other areas of focus will include the perceptions of different smells across different cultures and the connections between the olfactory sense and the other senses, with an emphasis on developing congruence between the senses.

The penultimate chapter of the book will center on the final sense, taste. The connections between taste and smell and between taste and vision will be explored in depth. The science behind the design of food will be discussed in connection to taste buds and the nature of how tastes are perceived by the brain. Various measures of quantity will also be considered in connection to food as well as perceptions of quantities that have been consumed. As with the other senses, the focus will be on how scientific findings have been and can be applied in product design.

Finally, the book will finish with a conclusion that summarizes the most important takeaways from the text and revisits some of the examples mentioned in this chapter in light of those takeaways. Avenues of future research will be discussed as well as ongoing initiatives and studies in the world of sensory marketing. In addition, several recent debates and controversies regarding sensory marketing will be explored and cutting-edge products with sensory aspects will be brought to the forefront in an effort to highlight current trends in sensory marketing.

Chapter 2

VISION

BLINDNESS AND SEEING: THE POWER OF VISION

Apple is a company that has used visual components extensively in the design of its products and advertisements. The company's logo consists of the picture of an apple with a bite taken out of the right-hand side and with a curved leaf on top. This shape is recognizable as Apple's logo even when it appears in different colors or when it is made to cover the face of a man in a bowler hat in a laptop art decal that parodies a work by French artist René Magritte. Apple has also appealed to vision in its advertisements for the iPod, which have included the images of dark silhouettes against brightly colored backgrounds and pictures of iPods in different colors to form a virtual iPod rainbow. The shape of the iPod itself is visually distinctive; if I were to place the shape of an apple on a Walkman, it would appear out of place, and if I showed most people the shape of an iPod, they would be able to recognize it not just as a device for listening to music but as Apple's music listening device. Thus, Apple has appealed to the sense of vision to make its products stand out in an increasingly large and diverse market of technological gadgets.

Literature offers a different look at the power of sight, or the lack thereof. For example, in his novel *Blindness*, the contemporary Portuguese author José Saramago describes a town whose inhabitants contract a disease that causes them to lose their sight—all are afflicted except for the wife of the main character, a doctor. The book is about how quickly the epidemic causes society to collapse, with many people driven to commit murder and theft while others are driven to despair and even to commit suicide. An earlier story on the subject was "The Country of the Blind," which was written by the more well-known author H. G. Wells. The narrator of "The Country of the Blind" encounters an isolated South American village whose inhabitants are all blind. Their customs are functional, albeit primitive, and people rely on their other senses to make up for their lack of sight. The narrator is struck by how limited the blind peoples' lives are, and he eventually flees when they try to remove his eyes in an attempt to correct what they believe to be a strange and dangerous defect.

What both Apple's ads and the above-mentioned literary works have in common, more than anything else, is that they illustrate how strongly most people rely on their sense of sight. It is no wonder, then, that the majority of sensory marketing, and even of marketing in general, has until quite recently focused on the sense of sight. Some of this can be attributed to the prevalence of primarily visual media, such as print, billboards, and, to a great extent, television and the Internet. However, it is also partially due to the power of visual sensory signatures as highly memorable and identifiable. To illustrate this point, look at these visual sensory signatures below and try to figure out what company they are associated with.

I hope you recognized several of the pictures and could associate companies with a portion of them. While the pictures were selected to represent some of the best-known

Figure 2.1 Vision Visual 1—Popular Logos and Symbols.
How many of these visuals do you recognize? How many can you associate
with a specific company?

visual sensory signatures, there are many, many more
famous images most people can recognize. The prevalence
of visual sensory signatures, which include logos, colors,
patterns, shapes, designs, and pictures, is extensive. For your
information, the pictures are associated with the following
companies, in order: McDonald's, Target, Starbucks, KFC,
Wendy's, Lacoste, Green Giant, Ralph Lauren, and Captain
Morgan.

While the sheer volume of visual sensory signatures does
hint at the importance of the sense for marketing, another
clue comes from the importance of sight for activities normally associated with the other senses. We are surprisingly
reliant on sight to identify the sources of sounds, to tell

different foods apart, and to be able to know what and where we wish to touch. Though this may appear to be far-fetched, try to perform some simple tasks with your eyes closed. For most people, it is quite challenging, for example, to take a shower, to get dressed, or to prepare a piece of buttered toast without using their sense of vision. The importance of vision in our everyday lives, in our work, and in our leisure activities is undeniable.

The rest of this chapter will provide an overview of how the sense of sight works, examining both sensation and perception of visual stimuli. The first section will discuss how the perception of visual stimuli can be manipulated. From there, the bases of visual sensory signatures will be explored, showing how diverse their building blocks can be. The later portions of this chapter will discuss several interesting phenomena in visual marketing, such as package design and the impact of geography and culture on the perception of color. While the exact nature of visual aesthetics and the study of all forms of visual advertising are beyond the scope of this book and of my research, I will touch on some principles from both of those fields to support my conclusions.

THE SCIENCE OF A SENSE

In the grand scheme of things, vision is a surprisingly narrow sense. Light is only a small part of the electromagnetic spectrum that we can detect with the human eye. It spans wavelengths approximately between 390 and 750 nanometers. Wavelengths of 400 nanometers correspond to light of a violet shade while wavelengths of 700 nanometers correspond to a shade of bright red. Green lies at about 500 nanometers, and the yellow shades usually are at values slightly below 600 nanometers.

In the eye, light is projected through the cornea and the lens onto the retina, which lines the back of the eye. The retina can perceive light because it contains two types of receptors, cones and rods, that convert the photons from light into electric signals that can be processed by the brain. The classic conception of cones and rods is that cones are what we use to see during daytime, and rods are what we use to see during nighttime. This is only partially true; both cones and rods undergo what is known as dark adaptation, which increases their sensitivity in a darker environment. The adaptation of cones is quicker than the adaptation of rods, and, as a result, if we are in a dark room, we will at first use primarily our cones. However, the adaptation of rods, while it takes more time, provides greater sensitivity to light than the adaptation of cones; that is, after about 5–7 minutes in a dark room, we will primarily use our rods.

A more accurate definition of the difference between cones and rods is based on the portions of the visible light spectrum to which each of those receptors is more sensitive. The sensitivity of rods peaks at around 510 nanometers, which corresponds to a light shade of green, while the sensitivity of cones peaks at around 570 nanometers, which corresponds to a light shade of yellow. This accounts for the relative "brightness" of foliage at dusk; due to dark adaptation, rods will be the primary receptors in use then, and, as a result, greens will be perceived more strongly. Another way to demonstrate this effect, which is known as the Purkinje shift, is to close one of your eyes for about 10 minutes and then to look at a blue object first with one eye and then with your other eye. Especially compared to your surroundings, the blue object will appear brighter to the eye that has undergone dark adaptation.

However, rods have less visual acuity. Acuity refers to the ability to carefully distinguish details. If I asked you to focus on any letter in this text, you would place that letter in the middle of your field of vision. Why? Because you would automatically want to align that letter so it can be perceived by the central area of your retina, the fovea, an area that contains only cones. This allows you to perceive a greater level of detail of the letter. This also explains why when looking for someone in a crowd, you move your eyes over the crowd to "pick out" the person with the cones in your fovea.

But what does all this mean for marketers? This is not such an easy question to answer. There are some simple applications, such as using more shades of blue than shades of red in an advertisement if the target audience has undergone dark adaptation, possibly because the audience has just been asleep or is in a movie theater. However, many applications deal not only with the sensation of light but also with the perception of light. To better understand how light is perceived, we must delve further into the workings of the human brain.

ILLUSIONS AND BIASES

In the opening chapter, I presented several optical illusions to illustrate the difference between sensation and perception. While it is easy to attribute the power of those illusions to that difference, there are several proven biases that underlie the construction of the illusions. First, let's look at the Ponzo illusion, reprinted on the next page. The two vertical lines provide perspective, giving the illusion of depth. This means that even though the two horizontal lines are the same size, we perceive the one on top as larger because we perceive it as closer to us.

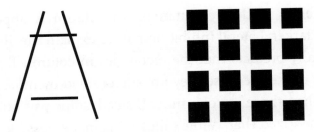

Figure 2.2 Optical Illusions (Ponzo and Hermann Grids).
Try out these optical illusions. Which horizontal line looks longer? What color squares do you see?

Another illusion you may be familiar with is known as the Hermann grid. It consists of sixteen large black squares separated by white space. Note that there are no gray squares at the intersections between the black squares—at least none are printed on the actual page. Try focusing on any one of the gray squares and notice how fast it disappears. Then move your eyes to any other part of the illusion, and the gray square will come back. It's a rather mind-bending illusion because even if you know that it's an illusion, you can't get the gray squares to go away. The Hermann grid works because of lateral inhibition, a process by which visual receptors temper the strength of their signals based on the signals that their neighbors are sending. In each of the intersection zones in the Hermann grid, lateral inhibition from the white areas found directly above, below, to the left, and to the right of the zone causes the appearance of the gray squares.

Another illusion that involves shades of colors is named White's illusion after its developer. Reprinted on the next page on the left, the rectangles in columns A and B are exactly the same shade of gray. If you want, you can cover up the black areas with a sheet of white paper to prove that the rectangles are the same color. Of course, they are perceived as different, with the rectangles in column A appearing much darker. Lateral inhibition fails to explain this illusion; it actually predicts that the rectangles in column B would appear darker because they are surrounded by more white space than those in column A. Instead, some psychologists have theorized that White's illusion is made possible by an idea of belongingness. In other words, because the rectangles in column B appear to "belong" to a longer horizontal black bar, they are perceived as lighter by contrast than the rectangles in column A, which appear to "belong" to the white bar instead.

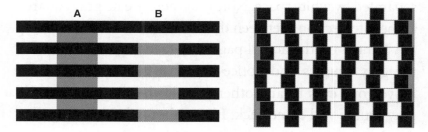

Figure 2.3   Optical Illusions (White's and Netlogo).
Try out these optical illusions. Which color rectangles look darker? Are the lines straight or crooked?

A final illusion to consider is the Netlogo illusion, which is found above and to the right. The rows of boxes in this picture are actually in a perfectly straight line. Of course, the ends appear to bend, giving the illusion of the boundaries being curved. The Netlogo illusion is a little different from the two previous illusions because it doesn't involve a shade of color but rather concerns the "straightness" of a series of lines. The Netlogo illusion works because the squares are not perfectly aligned with each other vertically, and this creates the impression that they are bent as the mind compensates and attempts to straighten the columns of boxes.

Based on my research on illusions, I have identified several consistent biases that are meaningful from the perspective of the marketer. A *bias* is any consistent misalignment between sensation and perception. Such biases, while they may not be shared by everyone, tend to hold true across cultures, age groups, and genders, even among people whose profession or experience would suggest that they would be immune to them. I have grouped the visual biases I will discuss into three categories: the direct distance bias, the sizing bias, and the consumption bias.

DIRECT DISTANCE BIAS

The first bias I have identified is the direct distance bias. The direct distance bias arises because the human brain perceives the shortest distance between two points to be the length of a straight line between those points even if the shortest path between them is specified to be otherwise (for example, if there is an obstacle preventing one from traversing the shortest linear path).[1] This happens because the mind uses the straight line distance as an anchor, and this anchor persists even when the straight line distance cannot be traversed. For example, consider a mall with many passages between stores that often intersect at strange angles or are even curved. When people are asked which of two paths of equal length is longer, they will overwhelmingly respond by selecting the path that has the shortest direct distance. This bias also works when people are asked to walk the two paths rather than merely visualizing them on a piece of paper.

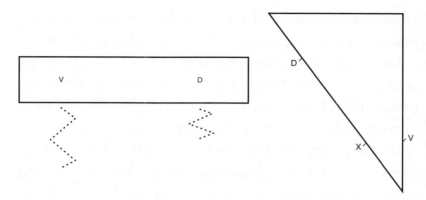

Figure 2.4   Direct Distance Bias.
In the figure on the left, assume each dot in the line represents one person. Which line is shorter? V or D?
In the figure on the right, assume you are at point X. Walking along the edge of the triangle to either point V or to point D, which point is closer?

The applications of the direct distance bias are numerous. Returning to the mall example, companies often want to locate their stores in areas that are close to certain central areas or certain other stores, such as a food court or a department store. In choosing the location of stores, it is important to keep in mind not only the actual walking distance mall patrons will have to traverse to get to the store but also the direct distance between the store in question and the other location. This applies also to proximity to parking structures; when people consider how far their car is from a certain store, the direct distance is just as important to consider as the actual distance.

Another application of the direct distance bias comes in designing the layout of lines. In many establishments, such as banks, grocery stores, or amusement parks, lines are cordoned off by ropes arranged in a zigzag pattern or in such a way that the line will snake back onto itself. One reason to do this is to utilize space as efficiently as possible. A different reason is to minimize the perceived length of the line. When people perceive a short direct distance between themselves and the end of the line, the line appears shorter than if the direct distance were longer, even if the two lines are of equal length.

SIZING BIAS

The second bias I have identified is the sizing bias. The sizing bias stems from the inability of the human mind to accurately calculate area, volume, weight, and size. Because we are unable to instantly know those quantities, we focus on one or more salient dimensions of the objects whose area or volume we wish to discover.[2] A simple example of this bias can be discovered with the help of the diagram below. Look at the three circles. What is your estimate of their relative size? How much bigger is the middle circle than the one on the left? How much bigger is the right circle than the one on the left?

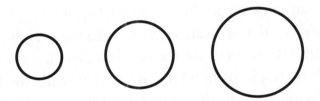

Figure 2.5 Three Circles.
Look closely at these three circles. What do you think their relative size is? How much bigger is the middle one than the one to its left? How much bigger is the one on the right?

The real diameters of the circles are in the ratio of 1 to 1.5 to 2. That is, the middle circle is 2.25 times larger than the one on the left, and the right circle is 4 times as large as the left circle. Most people vastly underestimate the areas of the two larger circles when compared to the circle on the left. In fact, the average of peoples' answers usually comes close to the actual ratios of the diameters of the circles. What this suggests is that people are using the diameters of the circles to estimate their areas. This is an example of a sizing bias because a different, more salient metric, in this case the diameter, is being judged in place of area or volume, which the human mind is unable to calculate quickly.

As you may have guessed, the sizing bias also applies to judgments of the volume of various shapes. While an obvious example of this could be formulated by asking people to estimate the volumes of three spheres, much as with the circles, more concrete, practical studies have been done to examine this phenomenon. In one study, I asked people to judge the relative volumes of two glasses, one tall and thin and the other short and wide. In reality, the two glasses were of equal volume. People consistently said that the taller, thinner glass had the greater volume. This is because when we see a glass, we estimate its volume based on two metrics, its height and its width, and we give them roughly equal importance in our estimate. However, if you recall the formula for the area of a cylinder, the radius (which corresponds to width) is squared while the height only factors once in the equation. When we estimate the volume by judging the height and width of the glass, we are actually undervaluing the contribution of the width to the volume, much as in the case of the three circles where we undervalue the contribution of the radius to the area.

There are many applications of the sizing bias in marketing and product design. Regarding the area bias, the circular product that comes to mind is a pizza. When pizza companies develop their sizing plans and pricing schemes, they often do not take the sizing bias into account; in this case, the bias makes people feel that, by comparison, small pizzas are larger than they really are and that large pizzas are smaller than they really are. This could allow pizza companies to charge extra for smaller, personal-size pizzas because people would be unaware of how much smaller the pizza is simply by looking at it or by considering its diameter. Conversely, they may not be able to make as much money off larger pizzas. The bias is also relevant in the design and pricing of other circular products such as tires, rings, coins, and plates.

The volume bias is relevant as well. In light of the study of the shapes of glasses, restaurants wishing to make their drinks appear bigger would want to use tall, thin glasses. On the other hand, restaurants wishing to make their drinks seem smaller—for example, if they were targeting dieters or calorie-conscious diners—would prefer to use shorter, wider glasses.[3] The bias is valid for similarly shaped objects, such as ice cream cones, milk jugs, and juice bottles. All of these objects have width and height components, and the human mind overvalues the height characteristic compared to the width characteristic when assessing their volume.

CONSUMPTION BIAS

The third bias I have identified is the consumption bias. By the consumption bias, I am referring to the amount of a given product we feel we have consumed. For example, after you finish a glass of water, how much do you think you have drunk? Or after you eat a plate of food, how much have you eaten? This type of bias is different from the direct distance and sizing biases because it is not entirely visual, but I have included it in the visual section because it usually works in conjunction with a visual stimulus.

For example, take the previously discussed scenario in which subjects were asked which of two glasses holds more water. As you may recall, one glass was taller and thinner, and the other was shorter and wider, but in reality both held the same amount of water. When I asked subjects how much water they had drunk after finishing one of the glasses of water, their responses were the opposite of their initial perceptions; subjects who drank from the shorter, wider glass felt like they had drunk more than subjects who drank from the taller, thinner glass.[4] At first, this seems counterintuitive because the same subjects had just claimed that they thought the taller glass held more water than the shorter glass. Why would they contradict themselves?

In reality, these results are not at all contradictory. The explanation lies in the expectations that are created when the subjects perceived the two glasses of water. When the subjects drink from the glasses, they consume an equal amount of water in both cases. However, when they drink from the taller glass, they expect a greater amount of water than when they drink from the shorter glass. When they finish, they are surprised at how much water was in the shorter glass, and this causes them to feel that they have drunk quite a lot of water. On the other hand, they are surprised at how little water was in the larger glass, and this causes them to feel that they have drunk a paltry amount of water.

The consumption bias can apply to more than glasses of water. When expectations are set up, such as by another visual bias, a size label, or a quantity measure, people will anticipate consuming an amount equal to their expectations. When those expectations are not met, people will adjust their perception of the relative quantity they have consumed accordingly. This has far-reaching applications in the restaurant business and in the retail industry in general—in fact, wherever expectations of certain quantities can be established and then met (or not met).

THE USES OF HUES

One of the most prominent aspects of any visual sensation is color. As discussed in the opening section, a color in and of itself can act as a sensory signature, as with pink and the breast cancer movement or as with Tiffany Blue. Shoe designer Christian Louboutin engaged in a legal battle over whether his signature red-soled shoes are protected under the designation of a trademark. After rival company Yves Saint Laurent used a similar design, Louboutin claimed that Yves Saint Laurent had copied his intellectual property, and he took the company to court over the issue. While the red-soled shoes clearly represent a sensory signature, the legal standing of such a distinction is not so clear. However, there are many more uses for color than just employing it as a sensory signature. Color can be one of the most enjoyable and artistic expressions, whether it is used for aesthetic purposes in artwork or in product design. In addition, the perception of certain colors can cause specific and predictable reactions that can be used by marketers to establish a mood for a product, location, or advertisement.

One common misconception about color is that it is a property of certain wavelengths of light. Technically, there is no such thing as "red light" or "blue light"; rather, color is created by our perception of certain wavelengths of light. In our cones, there are three distinct pigments, each of which is designed to perceive light of a slightly different wavelength. The relative strength of those signals allows the mind to perceive objects of different colors. In some scenarios, colors can be distinguished by only two of the pigments, but in most scenarios all three are necessary. This was first demonstrated by two nineteenth-century physicists, Thomas Young and Hermann von Helmholtz, who showed that people could replicate any given wavelength exactly by manipulating just three wavelengths of light in differing quantities.

Another common misconception about color is that every color induces a different mood and aura when it is perceived. The problem with this idea is that many of our conceptions about color are cultural rather than physical. For example, the association of pink with baby girls and blue with baby boys is a cultural phenomenon, not a reflection of pink being a fundamentally feminine color or of blue being a fundamentally masculine color. Other associations are links that have been established by marketers, as with Tiffany Blue or pink and the breast cancer movement. Sports teams offer another instance of this where fans associate the colors of their favorite team with feelings of competition, loss, or victory. Of course, this is not due to any inherent properties of those color combinations.

The only scientifically proven relationship caused by color is the contrast between longer and shorter wavelengths relative to performance in various tasks. In general, shorter wavelengths, which are perceived as blues, are calming and relaxing, but longer wavelengths, which are perceived as reds, are more stimulating and exciting.[5] Studies have applied this principle to test-taking scenarios, in which subjects who were primed by looking at a blue page performed better on creativity-based questions whereas subjects who were primed by looking at a red page performed better on more analytical or detail-oriented questions. This could have interesting applications in the corporate world, where meetings might be held in red or blue rooms depending on whether creative or analytical skills are more desired.

Another interesting experiment using color is the Stroop test. Consisting of words such as "green" or "blue" written in a different colors of type, the Stroop test investigates whether the perception of the color of the letters or the meaning of the word is dominant. As it turns out, for most people the meaning of the word is dominant; in other words, when they are asked what color the word is, they answer with the color named by the word rather than with the actual color of the letters.[6] This suggests that the process of reading is more natural, or is faster, than the process of interpreting color. I will discuss more of the cultural implications of different colors later in this chapter, but for now I move to a different type of sensory signature, patterns.

PATTERNS AS SIGNATURES

Colors and logos are one type of sensory signatures; another class of sensory signatures consists of patterns. For the purposes of sensory marketing, I have defined patterns as repeating series of visual components that, by themselves, would not constitute a sensory signature. This means that a single stripe, column, logo, or symbol would not be classified as a pattern. However, a series of stripes or symbols could easily constitute a sensory signature.

A prevalent example of a pattern of stripes and symbols that constitutes a sensory signature is visible on the American flag. When it was first created, the American flag did not resemble its current version, in which the fifty stars represent the fifty states and the thirteen stripes represent the thirteen colonies. However, the basic patterns, such as the "stars and stripes" and the signature colors of red, white, and blue, have largely remained the same. Over the years, the American flag has moved from the realm of a logo or symbol to take on greater significance. Any product with the colors red, white, and blue carries a patriotic connotation, especially if it also incorporates a number of stars or stripes. This is what makes the colors and shapes a pattern; even when the exact image of the flag is not present, the feelings associated with the flag carry over simply from the patterns that are visible on it.

Two of the most recognizable commercial patterns that form sensory signatures are used in the fashion industry. The first belongs to Burberry. The Burberry checkered pattern consists of three vertical and three horizontal stripes that form nine darker squares at their intersection points. Burberry trademarked its pattern to help prevent forgeries and knockoffs from trying to infringe upon its market share. The trademark was held up in court as legitimate and differentiable from other plaid or checkered products made by other companies. Obviously, companies cannot trademark large numbers of patterns to which they have no historical right, but by the same token, they have the right to protect the profits resulting from the advertising and development expenditures of making a pattern well known.

Louis Vuitton also has a trademarked, notable pattern that consists of its logo interspersed with various clover-like shapes that repeat at definite intervals. The company's logo, which is recognizable and trademarked, is comprised of the letters L and V laid on top of each other, with the vertical portion of the L slanted to the right. While this logo is a sensory signature in and of itself, the pattern forms a separate signature even though it incorporates the LV logo. The pattern is recognizable as the Louis Vuitton pattern even when the logo is not discernible. The use of patterns has allowed Louis Vuitton and Burberry to develop a sensory signature that can identify its products from a greater distance than that is possible with a logo alone.

THE DESIGN OF SHAPES

Imagine an octagon. For simplicity's sake, it can be any size, but make sure that its edges are all about the same length and the sides meet at about the same angle; in other words, try to envision as close to a regular octagon as you can. Pick a color and assign that color to the octagon. What color did you choose? This is one of those questions to which there is no right or wrong answer. Now, if you did not assign the color red to the octagon, picture the octagon in red. What shade of red did you pick? Odds are that in the second scenario, if not already in the first one, you picked a shade of red very close to the one that appears on stop signs. This is because the shape of the octagon is, in its own right, a sensory signature of the stop sign because so few other objects in our everyday lives have that shape.

In the vodka industry, two of the leading companies have established sensory signatures through the shape of their bottles. For example, Absolut Vodka's distinctive bottle is tall and thin, with a curved top that leads to a circular neck. Smirnoff also has adopted a signature bottle shape; the company's bottle is tapered in its midsection with a slightly wider bottom and features a wider neck than the Absolut bottle. Even though both companies make many flavors and sizes of vodka, they both have tried to maintain their bottle shape regardless of size or color so that consumers can identify the shape of the bottle with the brand name.

Using bottles with a distinctive shape is not unique to the vodka industry. For example, the juice company Orangina's bottle is spherical, imitating the shape of an orange. Nesquick's milk products are sold in a distinctive plastic bottle that narrows toward the middle and has a large, plastic screw-on cap. The perfume company Jean Paul Gaultier is known for its unique bottle shaped like a woman's torso. Tea company Arizona packages many of its drinks in large aluminum cans, which several other companies have subsequently attempted to copy. Sometimes, it can be difficult to trademark a bottle shape if it cannot be shown to be uniquely identifying and innovative enough to distinguish it from generic types of bottles.

One company that has made full use of shapes as sensory signatures in the design of its products is Apple. Its iPod, as I mentioned previously, appeals to several senses and has a distinctive shape that Apple has trademarked. The rectangular shape of the iPod, the circular shape of the touchpad, the buttons, and the rectangular screen together constitute the product's sensory signature. While some competitors have attempted to compete with the iPod by providing a similar product, with many of the same features and designs—for example, Microsoft's Zune—they were unable to copy the exact shape of the iPod because of Apple's trademark. Despite the iPod's shape being an apparently mundane mishmash of rectangles and circles, it is nevertheless recognizable and is distinctive enough to be trademarked and thus legally protected.

A final, different example of shape as a sensory signature is the Hershey's Kiss. Hershey's Kisses are just ordinary Hershey's chocolate given a distinct shape. The shape is very distinctive and original—it almost resembles a cone, except that it is curved instead of straight and has a slightly tapered middle. The shape is also recognizable even without the presence of chocolate. If you were given a wooden model of a Hershey's Kiss, you would probably know what it was a representation of. In addition, the shape of the Hershey's Kiss includes a small strip of paper folded into the tin foil wrapping and protruding from the top like a flag that can be unfurled. The juxtaposition of that strip of paper with the foil wrapping both contributes to the sensory signature of the shape of the Hershey's Kiss and also forms another important visual attribute of the product: its packaging.

PACKAGING AND CONSUMPTION

When consumers view goods to examine which ones they wish to purchase, they often view not the item itself but rather its packaging. This is especially true in places such as grocery stores or convenience stores, where most purchases are relatively cheap and not made with much (if any) deliberation. Aside from sensory signatures, though, there are certain trends in packaging that can convey specific attitudes and feelings about a product to consumers.

In academic settings, package design is evaluated largely based on the relative visible heaviness of products, that is, on how much weight, bulk, or density consumers associate with the product. Heaviness is chosen as the attribute to be examined because it is easy to see the relationships between packaging designs and heaviness. Whether it is heaviness or lightness that is the goal of package design is up to the developer of each package. For a low-calorie meal marketed to dieters, it would probably be best if the package conveyed an impression of lightness; for a rich, creamy meal marketed to body builders, it would probably be best if the package conveyed a sense of heaviness. Therefore, it is important to remember that heaviness is in no way synonymous with "correctness" or "incorrectness."

There are many ways to manipulate the perception of a product's weight through package design. One of the classic ways is through the positioning of the product's image on the package; product images that appear in the upper or left portions of a package convey lightness, while those placed in the bottom or right sections convey heaviness.[7]

Researchers are investigating whether the depth at which the image of the product appears impacts the perception of heaviness as well. They hypothesize that if the picture of the product is located in the foreground of the packaging, it will be perceived to be lighter than if the image is located in the background. Another possibility for changing the perceived heaviness of a product is to add motion to the picture of the product on the packaging.

Researchers are also looking at more subtle ways of influencing perceived heaviness based on their theory that if a consumer looks longer at the packaging, the product will gain perceived heaviness. That is, if a product's packaging is particularly engaging or puzzling or is designed in such a manner that the consumer will look at the packaging for more than a few seconds, the product may be perceived as heavier. This can also be simulated by adding a number of colors to the packaging or by making it more complex. Alternatively, if packaging is designed to be simpler so that the consumer's eye rests on it for a shorter period of time, the product may be perceived as lighter. I have included a picture showing several packaging designs. Which ones look heavier?

Figure 2.6a Snackwell's Cookie Packages.
Which of these packages look "lighter"? Which of these packages look "heavier"?

Credit: Xiaoyan Deng

Figure 2.6b   Market Pantry Cookie Packages.
Which of these packages look "lighter"? Which of these packages look "heavier"?

Credit: Xiaoyan Deng

A different aspect of packaging is its influence on consumption. Packages can be used to create expectations, which then serve as benchmarks when consumers actually consume a product. As explained above in connection with the consumption bias, these expectations can alter consumers' perceptions of how much they have consumed after they have used up the product[8] Variety in packaging can also serve to affect consumption. When the objects inside a package are more varied, such as different flavors of yogurt or types of chocolate, the rate of consumption will increase. Likewise, if the different types of the product are packaged in a random order or all together rather than in separate sections, rows, or containers, the rate of consumption will go up.

Packaging can become an art form in and of itself. There are a number of antique products that are known for their unique packaging. Several famous works of art, such as Norman Rockwell's pictures for the *Saturday Evening Post* or Margaret Bourke-White's picture of Fort Peck Dam for

Life magazine, became the visual identifier of how the magazines wanted to portray themselves to their readers. The covers of magazines serve as the "packaging" for the magazine because that is the only part of it consumers see as they pass by the magazine on a shelf or at a newsstand. A more recent example of packaging as art can be found in Mountain Dew's Green Label Art initiative, in which the company recruited several artists to design art prints to be placed on premium Mountain Dew bottles that were made of aluminum.

Packaging can also be used to mask unfavorable changes, such as downsizing, or to play up favorable changes, such as price decreases. This is accomplished by altering the primary attribute of the product that the packaging emphasizes. A package may have previously prominently displayed the fact that it contained 50 units of a given product, but after a downsizing to 40 units of product per package, the package now displays that the product lasts longer, performs better than its competitor, or has better ratings from a consumer group. Sometimes consumers are not even aware of a downsizing if the package is designed to hide the change, as with bottles whose bottoms have a bump that reduces the amount of liquid in the bottle. Package design, whether it is designed with the goal of conveying heaviness, increasing consumption, showing a piece of artwork, or hiding a change that consumers will not like, involves changing the way consumers visually perceive the package and the product.

CULTURES, COLORS, AND MORE

While most of the conclusions I have presented hold true across many different cultures, there are some important cultural differences that can interfere with supposedly universal results. For example, the idea of images in the upper left corner of a package conveying lightness has not been shown to be definitively true in Arabic countries or in other countries where the most commonly used script does not read from left to right or from top to bottom. Even some of the exercises in this book, such as the one in this chapter where I asked you to imagine a red octagon as a signature for a stop sign, would not necessarily have the same or any meaning in all countries. The octagonal shape is standard in most countries, but some countries, including Japan, use an inverted triangle shape for their stop signs instead.

Because discussing the numerous cultural differences in visual cues would fill this entire book, I will focus on differences in how color is perceived across different cultures. Some differences arise because certain companies that are active in only a few countries use the same color as a sensory signature. For example, in the United States, the color orange is not specifically associated with any one company, but in the United Kingdom it is associated with both a telecommunications company and an airline. Another example is the color of taxis. In the United States, the predominant color of taxicabs is yellow, which incidentally is the easiest color to identify due to the strength and intensity of its perception by the cones of the fovea. In Indonesia, however, most taxicabs are blue, in Romania most are white, and in Japan they come in all different colors.

Cultural differences can also manifest as discrepancies in hue preferences among people of different backgrounds. In particular, I want to examine whether a person's cultural background can be shown to influence what his or her favorite colors are. In a laboratory setting, subjects whose cultural background was either Chinese, Western, or some combination of both (such as a person of Chinese descent born in the Americas) were asked whether they preferred a red shade or a blue shade. Most subjects responded that they preferred the blue shade, regardless of their cultural background. While there was a slight difference in the degree of preference among participants, that difference was merely indicative of Westerners' tendency to express their preferences more strongly compared to people of a Chinese background and did not constitute a fundamental difference in hue preference.[9]

The study then examined how subjects would respond to cultural norms involving colors. This was accomplished by asking participants to choose a color of wrapping paper for a gift to give to a family friend or relative for a particular holiday. When a holiday such as St. Patrick's Day was chosen, people with a Western background picked green with greater frequency than did those of a Chinese background. When a holiday such as Chinese New Year was chosen, people of a Chinese background chose red with greater frequency than did those of a Western background (red is traditionally associated with the Chinese New Year and is held to be lucky during that time period as well). What this suggests is that cultural norms can influence people's color preferences when the norms are associated with a specific event, but, when they are not, the differences in preferences become far less pronounced.

The perception and meaning of visual cues such as colors and symbols can also change over time. The swastika, for example, is seen today as a symbol of racial hatred because of its use by the Nazi party. However, that is far from its original meaning. In the Indus Valley Civilization, which flourished many thousands of years ago, the swastika was used in prayer writings as a blessing, and in several East Asian writing systems it conveys the notion of "all" or "eternity." In fact, a careful examination of the swastikas of the Nazis and of the inhabitants of the Indus Valley reveals that, in the Nazi swastika, the direction in which the arms point is reversed. However, this does not influence the perceived meaning of the symbol. At various times in history St. George's Cross, which is today associated with England's national football team, has represented the monarchist movement in the Asian nation of Georgia, a Christian rebellion in Sardinia, and the coat of arms of Aragon.

CONCLUSION

Most of the marketing efforts in the twentieth century were visually oriented because of the prevalence of the primarily visual medium of print. While the development of television and Internet offers opportunities for auditory as well as visual marketing, the visual components remain of the utmost importance. Some of the simplest and most identifiable visual sensory signatures are logos. However, other types of visual sensory signatures also play an important role, such as colors, patterns, shapes, and symbols.

The difference between sensation and perception is especially notable when it comes to the sense of vision. The human mind can fool itself into believing many untrue things, and these biases can be identified and exploited by marketers. Some of the most important and prevailing biases are the direct distance bias, the sizing bias, and the consumption bias, all of which are relevant from the standpoint of consumers and marketers.

A different type of visual cue is produced by the packaging that accompanies a product. Packaging can be used to convey a visual impression of the heaviness of a product by displaying an image of the product on the bottom or right side of the package, by showing an image of the product in the background of the packaging, or by showing an image of the product in motion. Packaging can also be used to highlight certain attributes of a product or to hide other attributes based on which attributes marketers wish to emphasize or downplay.

Visual cues can be interpreted differently across different cultures. Some symbols have different meanings in different parts of world, and certain colors are associated with specific companies in some parts of the world and with other companies in other parts of the world. While there are some universal trends, such as red being as arousing and exciting and blue being thought of as relaxing and tranquil, many visual cues are dependent on the perceiver's culture, especially if they are associated with specific cultural norms or traditions such as holidays.

There are many connections between the sense of sight and the other senses. Many media, such as television and the Internet, appeal to both the sense of sight and that of hearing. For example, people use the sense of sight to judge the qualities of a plate of food before tasting it or even before smelling it. Vision also precedes touch, allowing us to identify which products we want to touch and what to expect when we feel them. Though vision is powerful and indispensable, it is also biased and predictable in a systematic way, two traits that give marketers plenty to work with.

Chapter 3

AUDITION

A WORLD OF SOUNDS

At the 2010 Oscars, Morgan Freeman was selected to hand out two of the lesser known awards, those for sound editing and sound mixing. Possessing a world-famous voice himself, Freeman narrated an action clip from the Batman movie *The Dark Knight*. He replaced the sounds and music that normally accompany the clip with commentary and descriptions of what was happening. The difference was startling. What had been an edge-of-your-seat chase scene had been transformed into something still artistic but also terribly boring. It lacked the vividness and intensity that had made the scene part of one of the top movies of that year. When the Oscars were awarded, the audience was aware of the great importance of sound editing and sound mixing in giving a movie a certain tone.

The story of the sound Oscars tells us something more subtle than just "sound is important" or "sound can change one's perceptions of an experience." It suggests that there are certain sounds, noises, pieces of music, or voices that are more appropriate in certain situations and that matching the sounds to the situations is as important as the presence of the sounds themselves. After all, Morgan Freeman's voice is not to be made light of; he is renowned as a narrator after doing work for some news programs and movies such as *March of the Penguins*. However well Freeman's voice could describe the hardships undergone by penguins in Antarctica, it did a poor job, or at least a poorer job than the music and noises produced by the sound editors, of accompanying the chase scene in *The Dark Knight*.

This concept, which I refer to as *congruence*, is one of the key aspects of understanding the impact of sounds in marketing. A certain piece of music or type of voice might be ideally suited for one objective but fail miserably regarding another. Most of the time, there is no universally "right" or "wrong" sound to use. Rather, the choice depends upon the target audience or customer and on what marketers think customers would like to hear. It is also essential to keep in mind that congruence depends on keeping sounds in tandem with the rest of the environment of a location (or film, as shown in the example of the Oscars). A store with a rainforest theme would hardly want to play rock music, and a store selling music albums would hardly want to play bird calls.

Sometimes, sounds associated with a particular experience or product are important to attracting customers. While whitewater rafting, it is customary for participants to scream and make lots of noise as they travel down the river. This is not necessarily because the noise makes the experience more enjoyable for the whitewater rafters themselves; rather, the sounds make the experience seem more exciting, unique, and terrifying for onlookers. Those onlookers are often the next group of potential customers, whether they are watching from the banks of the river or from the couch in front of their television sets. To see for yourself what a difference this makes, you can go online and watch a video of an extreme sport such as whitewater rafting. Then, watch it without sound. Which viewing was more exciting to you? Which one made you more likely to be willing to shell out money to participate in the activity?

Manufacturers of electric motorcycles face a similar challenge. The technology of lithium-based batteries for motorcycles is currently being developed, and crafting a fully electric motorcycle is something that may well be feasible in a few years. One of the main problems the product has faced, based on initial tests with motorcycle users, is that the noise of the machine is much different from that of a gasoline-powered motorcycle. Instead of a chugging or revving noise, electric motorcycles produce only a quiet, steady whir. You may think that this would improve the experience of riding the bike, but it has had the exact opposite effect and elicited negative comments of surprise, such as "What happened to the sound of the bike?" For most motorcycle users, the sounds of a motorcycle are part of the experience of riding it, and, while they may be perceived as obnoxious by bystanders, the bikers themselves enjoy them. In fact, Harley-Davidson even went so far as to try to trademark some of the sounds associated with its motorcycles and engines so that competitors could not imitate them exactly.

This chapter will further explore the role of music and voice in marketing and the concept of congruence. In addition, the associations between specific brands and certain sounds will be discussed together with brand name design and linguistic differences across cultures, and I will focus on the relevance of all this for marketing. As in the previous chapter, I will begin by discussing the actual workings of the sense of hearing (technically also known as "audition") in the ear and the brain, and I will conclude by revisiting some of the examples from the beginning of the chapter and highlight connections between hearing and the other senses.

THE EAR AND THE BRAIN

A classic question from philosophy asks whether a tree that falls in a forest where no one hears the noise will make a sound. While I will not try to answer that question from a philosophical standpoint, I will make a logical case for both sides of the argument. Technically, a sound wave is produced when the tree falls; thus, from the standpoint of sound as a sensation, a sound is produced whether anyone is there to hear it or not. However, the sound wave is not perceived by anyone, and thus, from the standpoint of sound as a perception, no sound is perceived. As with vision, it is important to distinguish between sensations and perceptions when it comes to the sense of hearing.

Sound waves have many physical properties that can be sensed by the ear. One such property is the amplitude of the wave, which is defined as the difference between the pressure value of the wave's peaks and troughs. Amplitude is measured in decibels, which are calculated using a logarithmic scale based on the sound pressure of the wave. A second property of sound waves is frequency, which measures how many cycles per second the wave goes through. A third property of a sound wave has to do with its harmonics; a sound wave can be combined with other waves that have related frequencies to form complex tones that repeat their patterns at some of the same frequencies as the original wave but are not exclusively formed by waves with the original frequency.

These properties directly correspond to our perceptions of sound waves. The amplitude, or decibel measurement, of a wave is perceived as the relative loudness or softness of the noise originating from the wave. The frequency of a wave is perceived as its pitch, which can vary from extremely high to extremely low based on our spectrum of hearing. The harmonics of a wave is perceived as the timbre of a sound. Timbre is what lets us differentiate between sounds that have the same loudness and pitch. While this may seem far-fetched, it is easy to show the differences by playing the same note on two musical instruments and comparing the two sounds. Even when the exact same note is played, most people can distinguish between a flute and a clarinet or between a violin and a cello; certainly, most people can distinguish between a piano and a trumpet.

As with vision, our ability to perceive sounds is actually quite limited. Human beings can only hear sounds between 20 and 20,000 Hertz (a commonly used unit of frequency). The hearing spectrum of dogs extends upward of 40,000 Hertz, a fact made use of by some collars and so-called invisible fences. Dolphins have a range of hearing that surpasses that of dogs in its upper range, and elephants can distinguish sounds well below 20 Hertz. One important point about the human hearing spectrum is that it is not uniform; for sounds closer to 20 and 20,000 Hertz, the decibel number has to be higher for us to perceive the sounds. Our power of hearing peaks between approximately 3,000 and 4,000 Hertz, and in that range we can distinguish even very faint sounds.

The human ear itself is divided into outer, middle, and inner regions. The outer region consists of the pinna, which is the external portion of the ear, the auditory canal, and the eardrum. When sounds enter the ear, they travel down the canal and vibrate the eardrum; this vibration is then transferred through a set of three small bones in the middle ear to the inner ear. Much of the inner ear is composed of the cochlea, a snail-shaped structure that contains the organ of Corti. Within the organ of Corti, small cells known as hair cells transfer signals to the auditory cortex in the brain, which then processes the signals into sounds.

Different portions of the auditory cortex are responsible for processing different attributes of a sound. Based on studies done on patients who lost certain hearing abilities, scientists were able to isolate areas of the cortex responsible for determining pitch, loudness, and the location from which a sound originates. In studies on musicians, scientists could also show that the auditory cortex is linked with memory; the musicians' auditory cortexes showed distinct improvement in pitch recognition over time compared to the auditory cortex in people who were not exposed to music as frequently.

As scientists begin to better understand the sense of audition, several implications of their research emerge for marketers and business people. While many of these ramifications concern the development of new products, such as cochlear implants that imitate the function of damaged or lost hair cells in the inner ear, an entirely different set of consequences concerns the use of sounds in marketing. The remainder of this chapter is devoted to looking at those implications and examining how they are put into practice.

SONIC BRANDING

I have defined the concept of linking a specific sound to a certain brand name as *sonic branding*. Sonic branding is basically just a specific type of sensory signature, one that appeals to the sense of hearing. While you may be able to think of some examples of sonic branding off of the top of your head, such as certain catchphrases or jingles that you associate with particular brands, there is a much greater variety of examples of sonic branding than you would expect. This is because sonic branding is not limited to words alone; noises and sounds, as well as phrases, can be used to form sensory signatures, sometimes even complementing each other.

Perhaps the simplest and most obvious form of sonic branding is the slogan, also known as a catchphrase or tagline. Slogans are phrases, usually short and expressive, that are associated with a certain brand. Although designed as part of a broader advertising campaign, slogans often live on and remain attached to the brand and sometimes have a longer lifespan than the original ad campaign. The objective of a slogan can vary. Sometimes, the goal is to create a consumer perception about a product or service, but many of the most successful slogans actually convey information about how to respond emotionally to a product or service rather than emphasizing any of its tangible attributes. Two prime examples of this are the slogans of De Beers and L'Oreal, which appear in the chart below. Another goal of a slogan can be to convey information, usually with a negative connotation, about a competitor, as in the Wendy's slogan found below.

L'Oreal: "Because You're Worth It"
De Beers: "A Diamond Is Forever"
Wendy's: "Now That's Better"
Skittles: "Taste the Rainbow"
McDonalds: "I'm Lovin' It"

Taco Bell: "Think Outside the Bun"
Cingular: "Raising the Bar"
Subway: "Eat Fresh"

A similar form of sonic branding is the jingle, a short song that appears in a commercial for a product or service. Jingles are usually light and up-tempo, with an emphasis on catchiness in the music and rhyme, meter, and rhythm in the lyrics. Some jingles can be very short, lasting only a few seconds. They are often inserted near the end of a commercial. One example of this is McDonald's "I'm Lovin' it" jingle, which resembles more a musical catch-phrase than a song. Other jingles are played during the entire course of a commercial, sometimes even making up the entire advertisement. This can be seen in a recent series of UPS advertisements that advocate the value added by solid logistics, claiming of various supply chain feats that "That's Logistics."

Both slogans and jingles include words, but, as I mentioned previously, sonic branding can be done without words. The most general type of wordless sonic branding relies on sound logos. Sound logos are any sound, series of sounds, or combination of sounds that are associated with a particular brand. One example of a sound logo is the lion's roar accompanying the visual logo of MGM Studios. Another example is the chime that is used by NBC. Both of those sound logos usually accompany visual images—for MGM, the roar is customarily shown with the lion moving its head around in MGM's visual logo, and for NBC the chime is often played in tandem with the company's pea-cock logo. If you are familiar with these sound logos, you may be able to hear them in your mind quite easily just by looking at or visualizing the image.

Sound logos do not necessarily have to accompany visual cues. In fact, Intel, a semiconductor chip manufacturing company, has built its entire brand name on a sound logo rather than a visual logo. You are probably familiar with Intel's sound logo, a four-note motif usually sung out something like "bum-bum-bum-bum." However, would you be able to visualize Intel's visual logo? In fact, do you even know what an Intel chip looks like? Would you even have known that Intel makes chips, rather than any other computer component, had that information not previously appeared in this paragraph? While some people will be able to answer yes to all three questions, most people do not have an eidetic memory and have never disassembled a computer. However, a good number of people who would answer no to all three questions would be able to recognize, if not reproduce, Intel's sound logo. This just goes to show how far-reaching a sound logo's effect can become when it is given the proper role in a series of marketing campaigns.

A final category of sound logos are those based on noises made directly by the product or service the logo is associated with. As discussed in the opening of this chapter, motorcycle manufacturer Harley-Davidson has attempted to trademark the noise produced by its bikes. This is an example of this type of sound logo. What sets logos such as that of Harley-Davidson apart is that they are not directly developed in advertising campaigns. Rather, they arise naturally with consumption or use of the product and become associated with that product in the mind of consumers. The only problem with this type of sound logo is that consumers often associate the logo with a general product category rather than a specific brand name, leading companies, such as Harley-Davidson, to become protective of the sounds (or sound logos) that their products make.

Multiple types of sonic branding can also be hybridized, as in the case of Snap, Crackle, and Pop, the mascots of Rice Krispies cereal. The three were originally cast based on a description of the cereal as it snaps, crackles, and pops when it is poured into a bowl of milk. Eventually, the trio was given formal names and cartoon faces and was associated with various songs, television shows, and marketing campaigns. While the trio does represent a sound made by the actual product, the three figures also represent other forms of the visual and sound logo. Interestingly enough, the names of Snap, Crackle, and Pop are changed in various parts of the world in order to better adjust to the cultural perceptions of the sounds that are generated by Rice Krispies cereal when it is poured into milk. This helps preserve the aspect of the trio as representing sounds made by the product itself. However, to a reader from an English-speaking country, referring to Snap, Crackle, and Pop as Cric, Crac, and Croc, or as Pim, Pum, and Pam, as they are called in French and Spanish, respectively, sounds a little silly.

In some instances, the goal of sonic branding is to foster brand recognition, as with Intel or NBC. The objective can also be to arouse a specific feeling associated with a specific noise generated by the product, as with Harley-Davidson and Rice Krispies. Sometimes the goal is to convey an emotion that is at best tangential to the product itself. No matter what the goal of sonic branding is, though, it is important to keep the objective of the sonic branding effort at the forefront, because the way in which the sonic branding is carried out can be just as important as the content it is designed to communicate.

VOICES AND SPEECH

One well-known instance of sonic branding is CNN's ubiquitous slogan "This is CNN," which appears at seemingly random intervals during breaks in many of CNN's programs. Unlike most sonic branding efforts, CNN's slogan does not really convey any information about the company's brand (most likely, you already know that you're watching CNN), and it also does not attempt to impart any particular emotion or mood in the listener. The slogan also does not target a competitor or evoke a sound associated in any way with the network. The reason for the choice of this slogan lies not in its wording but rather in the manner in which the words are spoken, specifically, in the speaker's voice: that of James Earl Jones. His voice carries a commanding, steadfast tone that garners respect, almost even fear. But why is this the case?

The answer lies in how our brain perceives speech. Two of the early researchers into speech problems and their causes were Carl Wernicke and Paul Broca. Regions of the brain that are today called Wernicke's and Broca's areas are the two primary parts of the brain responsible for processing speech; this is where the various parts of words we hear are processed and identified. These parts, known as phonemes, are the smallest units of language that cannot be

altered without changing the meaning of words. The number of phonemes in American English is generally held to
be in the forties, considerably more than the number of letters in the English alphabet due to the existence of different pronunciations of letters and certain combinations of
letters.[1] For example, the "s" in "pleasure" represents a different phoneme than the "s" in "sip," and the "u" in "but"
represents a different phoneme than the "u" in "put."

In perceiving speech, we perceive not only the spoken
phonemes but also several other characteristics of the
speech, such as its pitch, loudness, and rate. Rate here
refers to the number of words spoken in a given time
frame. We also perceive the way various phonemes are
pronounced, or sometimes confounded, and convert
the phonemes we hear into meaningful speech patterns.
While processing speech, we also form impressions about
the speaker based on some of the qualities I just mentioned (provided, of course, that the speaker is not a close
acquaintance).

Surprisingly, our impressions extend not only to physical
characteristics but to mental attributes as well. We make
predictions about the character of the speaker based merely
on factors such as pitch and rate of speech. Sometimes,
these predictions are hard to anticipate, and can be influenced by our own previous experiences as much as by the
actual attributes of the voice we hear. However, our predictions are more often accurate than not. We can even
predict physical attributes of a speaker quite accurately
independent of exactly which words were spoken.[2]

This has broad implications in the field of marketing.
Returning to the example of CNN and James Earl Jones, when
we hear James Earl Jones's deep voice, we naturally associate

it with such characteristics as authority and command. This is why CNN's slogan is so valuable; for news networks, it is important to be seen as having authority and being on top of the day's stories. In general, when we hear a male voice, we associate lower tones with power and strength, while higher tones are associated with weakness and stress.[3]

However, this is not necessarily the case for female voices. A study of female telemarketers showed that on average higher-pitched voices led to more sales than lower pitched voices.[4] However, many researchers do not believe this phenomenon to be universal. What is certain is that deep female voices do not suggest authority the way deep male voices do. In many ways, female voices are more complex than male voices because of the nebulous associations with "sexy" female voices. Some researchers have even theorized that certain voices are appealing because voice pitch is related to hormone production and serves as a signal of sexual readiness, even if the listener is of the same gender as the speaker.[5]

In addition to pitch, another important characteristic of a voice is the rate of speech. Studies have shown that listeners tend to conclude that speakers with higher rates of speech are more knowledgeable.[6] However, after a speaker is finished, listeners tend to retain more content if the rate of speech was slower. One possible explanation for this effect is that slower speech gives the listener more time to process and think about information as it is taken in; another possibility is that faster speech tends to cause listeners to zone out because they feel that too much information is presented to be able to comprehend it all at once.

It is important to consider what voice to use when creating a sonic branding strategy as well as what the voice will say. A deep, male voice conveys authority and power. A lighter, female voice could suggest a more playful nature. A fast talker causes the listener to feel more impressed and favorable toward the speaker, but this comes at the cost of listeners not being able to process as much information. For an advertisement where the reputation of the brand is of the utmost importance, it would be advisable to speed up the rate of speech, but for an advertisement where it is essential that listeners are able to remember information presented, it would be better to choose a slower speaker.

MUSICAL MUSINGS

Nowadays, our lives our saturated with music. Think about the number of songs (or, if you prefer, the number of minutes of music) you listened to yesterday. I'm not only talking about listening to the radio on the way to work or to your iPod at the gym, but also about hearing that familiar, yet still slightly awkward, tune that always seems to be playing in elevators, a badly distorted piece of classical music while you were on hold on the phone, the background music at the mall, that faint melody that was playing at your local coffee shop, or hearing the theme song of your favorite TV show. For most people, it's a surprisingly high amount, and that's not even counting the minutes of music that were playing during the advertisements for that TV show or during the commercials on the radio.

Because the motives and science behind all of the music that one listens to is beyond the scope of this text, I will focus on how companies use music. More specifically, I will look at why and to what effect companies use music outside of the field of sonic branding, which I have already discussed at some length. Just looking at the list of pieces of music mentioned in the preceding paragraph, it is easy to see how the music in the television and radio advertisements was specifically selected for its marketing appeal and implications. However, all of those examples (the elevator, mall, phone line, coffee shop, and TV show) consist entirely of music that was chosen by some company. Moreover, all those examples of music were deliberately chosen by someone in the company to be played to its "customers." This variety of tunes illustrates how the type of music that should be played can drastically change based on the target audience as well as the objective of the company representative, who, in this case, is acting, with or without his knowledge, as a sensory marketer.

Most uses of music in advertising consist of a tune that enhances the message of the advertisement rather than constituting the central message of the advertisement itself. Therefore, the congruence between the music used and the nature of the commercial is very important. Studies show that when congruence is achieved, music helps viewers of an advertisement better process its message.[7] For most people, this works because they would feel a very low level of involvement with the product or the advertisement without the music, and the music catches their attention. Ironically, for some people who are already very attached to the product, music can have the opposite effect and distract them from the message of the advertisement.

Another common use of music is as an ambient sound in stores. Ambient sounds are sounds that are embedded in an environment rather than in any one specific portion of that environment. When background music is played in a store, it can influence peoples' perception of the passage of time. Studies show that playing slower music causes people to spend more time browsing in a store than when music with a faster pace is played.[8] What is particularly interesting about background music is that its effects are completely subconscious; most people do not realize that they spent more or less time in a store because of the pace of the background music, and many people cannot even recall the existence or the pace of the background music after having left the store where it was played. Of course, it is essential to remember the importance of congruence when selecting background music as well—the potential benefits of background music only arise when people perceive the music as congruent with the environment of the store.

It is vital to understand the target audience when considering how companies use music. While it is easy to make generalizations such as "pop music would appeal to younger people" or "oldies would appeal to older people," it is possible to sharpen these statements in a more quantitative manner. In one study, people of different ages were asked to rate a variety of musical clips from different years.[9] The result resembled a normal distribution with the peak, representing the age of the respondents when their most favorable music was released, in their midtwenties. For example, this means that people born in 1950 are most likely to prefer music that was released in or otherwise associated with the 1970s. On the other hand, people born in 1990 are more likely to prefer the music produced currently than music that is either older or has yet to be produced.

Sometimes, music can be used as a way to keep out certain groups of people as much as to attract others. One historical incident of this occurred during Operation Just

Cause, the US invasion of Panama in 1989. After the United States forced the Panamanian dictator Manuel Noriega into a diplomatic building of the Vatican, the American forces continually blasted the building and Noriega's surrounding compound with loud rock music. While the US military has claimed that the purpose of the sonic barrage was to prevent the use of microphones and other listening devices, many analysts believe that the music played a key part in Noriega's surrender.

While I am by no means advocating a 24-hour regime of rock music to pester your annoying neighbors, similar tactics can be, and indeed are, used by several companies today. Retailer Abercrombie and Fitch deliberately plays contemporary music at a volume of around 90 decibels, only slightly below the legal limit for a workplace environment. This is comparable in volume to the continual buzzing of a chainsaw. While one purpose of Abercrombie and Fitch's music is to attract teens and young adults, the company's target market, the music also serves to keep away older people and parents. By keeping away older people, the company is better able to preserve its brand image of being young and cutting-edge. By keeping away parents, adolescents are less likely to be shooed out of the store, and they are out of range of the voices that usually advise them to be reasonable, if not stingy, in their purchases.

Classical music can have the opposite effect of the loud, contemporary music played by Abercrombie and Fitch. Some stores wishing to target older consumers have taken up playing classical music or opera in their establishments. Other businesses, such as some 7-Eleven stores, have taken up playing classical music outside their stores to discourage loitering. The trend has even been picked up by some municipal facilities, such as parks and subways, where playing classical music may reduce the number of homeless people, beggars, and crimes even if played only at a quiet volume.

A final trend I will discuss is the increasing number of partnerships between musical groups and companies that go beyond simply using the group's music in advertisements. When the image of a musical group fits well with the image of a brand, and it is perceived as congruent, the two can achieve a synergistic relationship. Starbucks has partnered with many artists to promote their career through in-store sales of compact discs, and in the process it has gained a reputation for building small names and stocking holiday-themed albums by contemporary singers. Victoria's Secret was the exclusive retailer for a greatest hits CD of the Spice Girls that was released in 2007. Both Victoria's Secret and the Spice Girls rely heavily on the image of sexy women for their success, and the two were perceived as going hand in hand. The Spice Girls even performed a reunion show during Victoria's Secret's annual fashion show. Such partnerships can benefit not only companies but also musicians, who can gain exposure to the customers of the company and sometimes can even pick up corporate sponsorship deals as well.

WHAT'S IN A NAME?

One of the most important auditory cues associated with any brand-name product is the brand name itself. The brand name is not really a sensory signature in itself or an example of sonic branding, but it still has the power to make or break a product line's success. Sometimes, a brand name may be perceived as lackluster, might be difficult for the consumer to pronounce, or it could convey a different meaning in a different culture, all of which could lead an otherwise well-conceived product line to fail. An example of this phenomenon was the Entire Butt line of porter beers introduced by the Salopian brewing company in Britain. In England, "butt" refers to a barrel, so the name of the beer refers to the variety of ingredients that went into the brew, but in America the word does not have that meaning. This creates an additional challenge for the company in marketing its product in America. This may seem funny to younger consumers and increase sales to them temporarily, but it presents a serious problem for the long-term sales of the product in the United States.

While some words or phrases, such as Entire Butt, have different meanings in different parts of the world, there are some universal preferences and associations for certain phonemes. The linguist Edward Sapir conducted a study in the 1920s showing that the "i" sound in "mil" is associated with smaller objects than the "a" sound in "mal" regardless of both the exact word in which the phoneme appeared and the cultural background of the participants.[10] A more recent study examined the attributes we assign to certain products based on the phonemes we hear in fictitious brand names.[11] The results, a brief version of which is included here, show that certain phonemes are perceived as more feminine, faster, and/or lighter than others. The study also explored other less tangible properties, such as the creaminess of ice cream, finding that "frish" was perceived as less creamy than "frosh," where the "i" in "frish" is pronounced as in "kiss" and the "o" in "frosh" is pronounced as in "chop." This would suggest that the selection of the brand name can convey a wide variety of nontraditional attributes, such as creaminess or smooth-ness, if it makes use of the correct phonemes.

Among the companies specializing in developing brand names are Lexicon, Strategic Name Development, and Name Stormers. Most of these companies are fairly small in terms of number of employees, but they often work for big-name clients to develop brand names for products to suit their needs. When developing a brand name for a product, these companies brainstorm a list of words that are somehow related to the product, attributes of the prod-uct, or emotions associated with the product. Then, they manipulate one or more of those words to make a brand name, keeping in mind the culture where the brand name will be used and the vowel-to-consonant ratio they wish the brand name to have.

The products Lexicon has helped name include well-known staples such as Swiffer, Blackberry, Febreze, and Dasani. Swiffer, which is a name attached to household cleaning products, conveys a notion of speed ("swift") as well as a notion of being greater than or better than some-thing else (the "-er" ending). Blackberry is a crisp, appealing name for a mobile device. Febreze suggests a breeze, which is itself associated with spring and cleanliness. Dasani makes use of the prefix "sani," which suggests cleanliness, as in the words "sanitation" or "sanitary." Lexicon makes use of word meanings and associations already established in our mind to craft brand names that make us think of the positive characteristics they try suggest to us—even though we may not be aware of the process.

Culture and geography play a key role in the percep-tion of brand names. As the above example of Entire Butt shows, sometimes certain meanings can be lost or gained when brand names move from one region or nation to another. Lexicon takes this into account when designing brand names; if a product brand name is to hold up in French-speaking or Spanish-speaking countries, then using a name with a Latin root can preserve the meaning across the language barrier. Sometimes, a company has to accept that it will not be able to maintain the same brand name in other areas of the world but must adopt a different name in different countries. For example, in Korea, the formal name of Starbucks is phonetically similar to the English word, but its colloquial name instead translates as "Star-Teahouse," a reflection of the differing preferences for tea and coffee in the Asian culture of Korea compared to the Western cultures where the brand name of Starbucks was developed.

Another interesting complication arises from the nature of feminine and masculine distinctions in various languages. In English, the word "the" is used universally as a definite article. However, in most Romance languages, such as French and Spanish, and even in German, the definite article varies with the gender of the noun it precedes. For example, in French, the definite article is either "*le*" or "*la*" depending on the gender of the noun, and in Spanish the definite article is either "*el*" or "*la*" based on the same criterion. When picking a masculine or feminine brand name in those countries, the name must be accompanied by the proper definite article; conversely, a brand name that incorporates a definite article therefore automatically assumes a feminine or masculine connotation based on the gender of the definite article. In Chinese, however, the definite article does not differ on the basis of the gender of the noun; in fact, until coming into contact with Western cultures, Chinese used the same word, "*ta*," to refer to both "him" and "her" regardless of the gender of the antecedent.

CONCLUSION

There are many different types of auditory sensory signatures. Companies use sound logos, jingles, slogans, and noises associated with their products to promote their brands through sonic branding. Music can play an important role in sonic branding and also has many other uses for marketers, whether it is incorporated into a song directly promoting a product or is just playing in the background while potential consumers shop at a store. The voice chosen for sonic branding is also important; deep masculine voices can convey a sense of confidence and authority, but a female voice is more likely to appear light and beautiful. The nature of language and speech perception presents an opportunity to design brand names that are associated with specific sentiments, but it is also possible to convey the wrong message if the sonic brand is executed improperly or if meanings change across cultural or geographic boundaries.

As the importance of sonic branding and of sensory marketing appealing to the sense of hearing in general is recognized, the need for better protection of auditory signatures becomes evident. However, the line between an auditory signature that can be trademarked and a sound that is associated with a product, rather than being a brand name, is sometimes unclear. Regarding the above-mentioned example of Harley-Davidson, Harley lovers would most likely assert that the sound of the motorcycle is distinctive to Harley bikes, but fans of other brands would insist that the sound of the motorcycle is common to all brands of bikes. They might even go so far as to associate the revving sounds of the engine with their personal favorite brand instead.

Another challenge of auditory-based marketing has arisen with the prevalence of Internet advertising. Television advertisements are expected to have sound, but many people surf the Internet with sound disabled. That is, only a fraction of the people who see an online advertisement will also hear it. Moreover, web surfers sometimes perceive sound as an annoyance, and this increases the likelihood that people will have a negative reaction to the sound accompanying an advertisement. A third problem is that, compared to television viewers, web surfers have much greater power to navigate away from advertisements. These challenges call for a different approach to crafting auditory signatures when the primary medium through which the signatures will reach consumers is the Internet rather than television.

Despite these problems, auditory signatures will continue to be prevalent. If Morgan Freeman's narrative voice and his stint at the 2010 Oscars tell us anything, it is that the technology that produces sounds and the science to understand how those sounds are perceived is continuously being developed and refined. As marketers come to contemplate and embrace these breakthroughs, sonic branding and the use of auditory signatures is sure to be on the rise in the future.

Chapter 4

SMELL

SCENTS OF THE PAST AND PRESENT

Imagine an ancient Egyptian temple as it would have looked three thousand years ago when it was frequented by priests and worshippers. What would strike you the most? What comes to mind? Some people would describe pictures of primitively drawn men and women; other people would picture a vast complex carved from granite and obsidian; yet others would focus on ceremonial objects like boats or figurines. The artwork would be beautiful, but focusing solely on the visual components of the experience of visiting an Egyptian temple would be leaving out a great part of the sensory experience.

What I think would be an equally stunning part of the experience would be the aroma. Egyptian priests were renowned for crafting unique, delicate, and rich blends of incense. Among the scents that would waft in on a breeze of hot air were green and white incense, both widely used in daily religious ceremonies. More exotic scents were encountered too, such as kyphi, which was a blend of local fragrances, and jb, a musky aroma that had a hieroglyphic representation similar to the hieroglyphic character for "goat."

Associating symbolic and religious meaning with scents was not unique to ancient Egypt. In the Bible, one of the gifts given by the three wise men was frankincense, which was a particularly valuable type of incense whose aroma was widely revered. Incense was also common in Hindu and Buddhist religious rituals, and it remains in use in some parts of the world to this day. Even through the

Middle Ages, the burning of incense was not uncommon in churches and cathedrals across Europe. Such fragrances were seen as a luxury the common people did not have access to except at religious gatherings, and so they took on a mystical significance.

Aromas also played an important part in many other cultures. Many Roman baths had a room called an unctuarium that was reserved for the storage and application of perfumes and other scents. In that role, aromas became a mark of class distinction because certain fragrances could only be afforded by the wealthy. An entire hierarchy of classes could be defined by how they smelled. In the Middle Ages, most people only had the opportunity of bathing once per year. Lords and ladies, who had the privilege of doing so more often, were able to show their status by avoiding the unpleasant smells associated with the peasantry. The trend of bathing practices as a distinguishing mark of financial classes continued well into the industrial era and even with the advent of indoor plumbing, which at first was a luxury reserved for the wealthy few. It is only recently that showers and baths have become a staple of most households.

Scents are also used to distinguish between genders. Some African tribes associate the smells of certain animals with men and those of other animals with women; the animals associated with each gender are those they work with every day, such as men with animals that are hunted and women with animals that are domesticated. Having different classes of perfume for men and women is an age-old practice in the Mediterranean world. For example, Cleopatra even infused the sails of her ship with her signature scent when she greeted Marc Antony after the death of Julius Caesar. Catherine de Medici, a powerful and long-serving queen of France, had a private perfumer whom she communicated with using a secret passage to make sure that no one could steal or copy the recipes of her perfumes.

Despite many changes since then, many of the traditional customs and attitudes regarding scents are still in place. A person with body odor is held to be unclean and slovenly, and a woman wearing the right perfume can turn the head of every man in the room. Not only do such perceptions about scents still exist, but marketers actively reinforce them. The sheer number of different fragrances, deodorants, and other scented hygiene products on the market bears witness to the vast business opportunity scented products present.

Scent marketing has also created further scent distinctions beyond gender and income. There is no longer one single scent for men or two for rich versus poor men; in fact, there are now many different scents for men of different age groups or lifestyles. The same is true for women. Marketing has brought scents to products that traditionally did not have aromas infused into them, such as foods, drinks, detergents, soaps, shampoos, face creams, crayons, and doctors' gloves. While it may seem that such uses of scents are wasteful or superfluous, they can act as powerful signatures of those types of products.

Given that nearly everything around us has a smell of its own, how are different scents recognized? How can a product's scent serve as a unique signature? To understand the answers to these questions, we first need to understand the olfactory process.

THE OLFACTORY PROCESS

It is a commonly known fact that dogs are far more sensitive to smells than humans are; canines are frequently used by police units to detect drugs and track criminals based on dogs' heightened awareness of odors, which is due to the great number of olfactory receptors dogs have. Whereas the average human has around ten million receptors, dogs can have as many as one billion.[1] What this does for canines, and for many other similarly equipped animals that depend more acutely on their sense of smell for survival than humans do, is lower the threshold at which a scent can be perceived.

A basic measure of the level at which a scent can be perceived is called the *detection threshold*, which is defined as the portion of a scent that needs to be present in the air for a person to be able to notice the presence of the scent. Usually measured in parts per billion, detection thresholds can vary from less than 1 to over 100,000 parts per billion depending on the scent. There is an important distinction between that detection threshold and the *recognition threshold*, which is the concentration at which a scent can be identified by such descriptors as "flowery," "sweet," or "rancid." The recognition threshold is usually significantly higher than the detection threshold, sometimes even as high as three times the concentration. At levels between the recognition and detection thresholds, humans can perceive the presence of a scent, but they cannot attach any meaningful descriptors to that scent.

Another challenge in scent perception for humans is identifying the specific source or sources of a scent. People may be able to identify a scent as "flowery," but it is considerably more difficult to say whether it is the scent of a rose, a daffodil, or a violet. Even for more common scents, such as those of an orange, a banana, and a lemon, it can be very difficult to identify the source when only the scent itself is present. This task of identifying scents becomes significantly easier when people are given a list of scents and are asked to match the scents they smell to those that appear on the list. Thus, the trouble would seem to lie in the inability of our memory to match scents with their sources rather than in the inability of our sense of smell to distinguish between specific scents.

The science behind how we perceive smells is actually quite complex. When odor molecules enter the nose, some of them are conveyed into the olfactory mucosa. This region is approximately the size of a dime and is located at the top of the nasal cavity. The olfactory mucosa is home to olfactory receptors, which contain neurons that send impulses to the brain. The impulses are then picked up in the olfactory cortex, which is also the site where different scents are identified.

Humans possess approximately 350 different types of olfactory receptors.[2] Each of these receptors fires signals to a different glomerulus in the olfactory cortex. The glomeruli are small, spherical bulbs that act as bridges between the olfactory nerve and the brain. The different patterns of glomerulus activation correspond to different types of scents. With 350 distinct receptors, there are millions of possible permutations of receptor activations, each of which corresponds to our perception of a specific scent.

The physiology of smell, however, does not explain why certain odors are perceived in certain ways. For example, why are we able to detect small differences in chemical composition only with certain compounds? Why is garbage usually perceived as stinky? Why is coffee aroma usually perceived as rich and appealing? While you may or may not agree with the perceptions of garbage and coffee I just mentioned, many people think of these fragrances in that manner. Surprisingly, most of these types of perceptions are not something we are born with; rather, they are learned or acquired. Sometimes, these perceptions are even influenced by the common perceptions of society or by those of our friends, family, and culture. The process of how we learn to associate certain emotions, feelings, and perceptions with specific scents is discussed in greater detail in the next section.

FORMING PERCEPTIONS OF ODORS

The notion that we consider perceptions of certain scents pleasant or unpleasant is called the *learned view* of odor preference.[3] It contrasts with the *innate view*, which states that odor preferences are hardwired in the brain. Regarding our sense of taste, understanding it as hardwired works quite well; for example, infants show clear preferences for sweet flavors and foods and distaste for bitter foods. However, that approach does not quite explain how the sense of smell works. Many of the scents that are supposedly universally unappealing are actually not at all perceived as unpleasant by newborns who have never been exposed to them before. More specifically, what is important is that the infants have never been exposed to other peoples' reactions to these scents before, so they have not yet learned what is considered the proper response.

This has been shown in several studies that monitor the behavior of infants when exposed to certain scents, such as those of feces or urine.[4] Infants do not show the disgust that would be expected of an adult. Even infants' reactions to specific chemicals, such as those found in certain fruits or in spoiled foods, are vastly different from those of adults. For example, infants do not show aversion to the scents of rancid meat or dead animals, smells that are generally held to carry universally negative connotations. It is precisely the existence of those connotations, though, that drives odor preferences in adults who have been exposed to and internalized the socially acceptable responses and preferences for certain scents.

The learned view of odor preferences is based on the concept of *associative learning*. Associative learning is the process by which we come to associate certain experiences with feelings.[5] For instance, if people generally experience the smell of lavender when they are getting a massage, then that fragrance will become associated with relaxation. If they subsequently encounter that fragrance outside of a massage parlor, it can still evoke feelings of relaxation.

The linkage due to associative learning has been studied in many different settings. One study looked at how people perceived a smell that is found in the chemicals present at dentists' offices. People who had a particularly bad experience with a dentist in the past found the smell far more unappealing than people who had not had such a negative experience.[6] Sometimes, this phenomenon can also underlie cultural differences in the perception of certain scents. A study conducted in the 1960s found that wintergreen was perceived as disgusting in the United Kingdom, but in the United States it is perceived as likable.[7] The reason for this was eventually postulated to be the use of chemicals smelling like wintergreen in British hospitals during World War II, which led British people to link the smell to the negative experiences and suffering they had undergone. In the United States, no such associations exist; rather, the smell of wintergreen is usually associated with candies, and therefore the perceptions are far more positive.

Studies have also examined the connections between odors and concepts other than just "positivity" or "negativity," even going far as to create and then observe those linkages in the laboratory. In one study, several children were given an impossible task while exposed to an odor usually considered neither likable nor unpleasant.[8] Then, while exposed to the same odor, they were asked to perform a series of small tasks requiring them to concentrate on solving various types of problems. The children in that group did considerably worse than those in another group who had not been exposed to any scent at all. They also did worse compared to a third group who were exposed to a different scent during the second series of tasks.

The children's poorer performance can be explained as a result of associative learning. During the initial task, the children learn to associate the scent they are exposed to with emotions such as frustration and irritation. That connection persists the second time they are exposed to the scent. In a similar study with college students, people who were exposed to the scent during both series of tasks showed behaviors during the second task such as giving up quickly, spending less time on difficult tasks, and diminished patience.[9] The connection between odors and emotions that is built through the process of associative learning can have a significant effect on performance in tasks. It is also relevant from a marketing standpoint because it suggests that certain emotions could be elicited in potential customers based on the presence (or absence) of certain scents.

The innate view of odor perception is also refuted by the fact that perceptions of odors are very easily manipulated with external cues. Depending on the label given to a particular scent, it can be perceived as being very appealing or very unappealing. When people are exposed to a smell that is labeled "vomit," they are very likely to view the scent as undesirable and disgusting. When the same smell is labeled "parmesan cheese," perceptions are much more positive.[10] This holds true even when the smell is that of parmesan cheese; it is the label of the smell and not the smell itself that causes perceptions to change. When the same set of people are exposed to the same smell, but presented with a positive rather than a negative label, many of them will claim that the smell is likable, appealing, and originating from a source they would like to consume.

This indicates that marketers could mask unpleasant odors by appropriate labels or convince consumers that scents associated with particular products have certain properties simply by describing them as such. The same approach can also be used to cover up mistakes; for instance, a French company was surprised to discover that, after shipping two batches of energy drinks in the wrong boxes, almost no one complained. Consumers were so convinced by the labeling of the drinks that, even after smelling and tasting the drink, they failed to notice that they had consumed the wrong product.

There is some evidence, however, for a hardwired link between certain scents and particular responses. For example, when exposed to the scent of a predator, many animals become agitated and attempt to flee even when they have not been previously exposed to that scent. In addition, responses to pheromones are encoded genetically; that is, the biological response to them, which is important in mating, does not require any learning. Such responses to scent are often associated directly with survival, reproduction, and other functions essential to the continuation of the organism's life.

MEMORIES AND MORE

The notion of a connection between smell and memory is nothing new; the French author Marcel Proust, working around the turn of the twentieth century, wrote in his seven-volume series *Remembrance of Things Past* about a series of memories triggered by the aroma arising from dipping a madeleine biscuit in his tea. He found that the scent triggered his memories (or his "Remembrance") in especially vivid detail, allowing him to narrate many stories that occurred when he was younger. Possibly due to the richness of Proust's prose, the idea that an aroma can evoke a particularly poignant memory became accepted as truth. Surprisingly, this idea is not entirely false, and I have conducted scientific research that supports the anecdotal link between smell and memory.

The Proust Phenomenon can be easily seen in people who are exposed to cues that remind them of their childhood. While a picture of a toy or the feel of the toy may be able to remind people of their childhood, no other cue is as potent as a scent-based cue. In my studies, I have found that for most people the smell of playdough is sufficient to trigger memories from their childhood. If you don't believe it, try it for yourself! If you used to play with playdough at all as a child, just opening a small tub of the dough and taking a whiff will "send you back" to your childhood with far more vividness than looking at a picture of your childhood home would be able to do.

In one study, I examined the connection between smell and memory by exposing half the participants to pencils that had been infused with the scent of an essential oil and the other half to unscented pencils.[11] While the pencils were in view, all participants read the same list of eleven attributes of the pencils. Many of these were claims that could possibly be part of an advertising campaign for pencils, such as being environmentally friendly, easy to sharpen, or longer lasting. Then, after several fixed time periods of 5 minutes, 24 hours, and 2 weeks, the participants were brought back and asked to list as many attributes of the pencils as they could. The people who had been exposed to the scented pencils showed significantly better ability to recall attributes of the pencil than those who had seen the unscented pencils. In the Proust phenomenon, the scent, when reintroduced, brought back memories. However, my research went beyond the Proustian phenomenon. Not only did memory improve with reintroduction of the scent; it also improved without scent reintroduction. While there was better memory for the scented (versus unscented) pencils after all three time intervals, the improvement was most drastic two weeks after the initial exposure: people were able to recall more than three additional attributes (of the original eleven) without scent reintroduction and nearly six additional attributes with scent reintroduction. In comparison, people exposed to the unscented pencils recalled fewer than one attribute.

This study represents an advance in establishing the connection between smell and memory because it showed that when a scent is linked to certain details (such as the attributes of a pencil), a repeat exposure to that scent not only activates a link in the mind to the product but also can increase the mind's ability to remember other details about the product. Equally important was the finding that people who were given scented pencils recalled more attributes of the pencil even when the scent was not reintroduced at the time of recall. This suggests that scents aid not only in the process of retrieval but also in the process of encoding memories in the brain. This means that being exposed to a scent actually boosts memory regardless of whether or not one will later encounter the scent again. It also suggests that scent-based signatures could be more potent than visual or auditory signatures when the primary purpose of the signature is to help consumers recall attributes of a product.

This research has been used by many firms selling scented products on their websites and in their promotional materials. They can now claim that their product not only smells better than competing, unscented ones, but also that studies have shown that scents can help people remember associated details and features.

This close link between smell and memory is due to the structure of the human brain. The olfactory bulb is contained in the limbic system along with the amygdala and the hippocampus. The amygdala is known as the center of emotions, and the hippocampus is involved in the

processing and formation of memories. The three structures are only a few synapses away from each other, so the
connection between smell and memory is thus physical as
well as conceptual. From Proust's madeleine to present-
day laboratories, the link between scent and memory is a
powerful and poignant tool whether it is used for the sake
of narration, in science, or in business.

SCENTS AND CULTURES

One of the implications of the learned view model of scent
preferences is that peoples' opinions about different scents
are influenced by their background. Part of this background
is personal, as with the example of peoples' reactions to the
smell of chemicals found at dentists' offices, and part of
this background is historical, as the example of the different reactions to wintergreen in Britain and the United
States has shown. Another part of this background is cultural; that is, the society we grow up in can be as important
in shaping our scent preferences as the above-mentioned
other types of experiences.

An easy way to see this is to consider the scents we associate with "home." What scents do you associate with your
home and your childhood? For most people, these scents
are considered positive and seen in a nostalgic light, often
with great fondness. Some of these scents are linked to specific activities of childhood, as seen in the example of the
smell of playdough. One scent that is fairly universal in its
appeal is "Mom's home-cooked meal," which is linked to
the emotional sense of being at home as well as to memories
of eating with one's family in one's youth.[12] However, what
exactly constitutes "Mom's home-cooked meal" varies

drastically from person to the next, reflecting not only food preferences but also cultural differences. Therefore, it is difficult to tap into the appeal of home-cooked meals by using only one scent. The scent of a turkey dinner may not at all evoke a sense of home for people of Asian descent, and similarly the smell of salted fish or curry may be perceived as undesirable by people of Western origin.

Sad occasions are also associated with various scents. When asked to associate a scent with the feeling of sadness, most respondents think of scents associated with an illness or a funeral, but the specific scents differ from culture to culture. For instance, porridge is served at Chinese funerals, and as a result the scent of porridge represents sadness for many Chinese people. However, the smell of a funeral pyre may evoke the most sadness for Hindus. Similarly, happiness is often associated with weddings, but it may be associated with the smell of incense in one culture and the smell of a certain flower in another. Scents people associate with sadness or happiness cannot be generalized because they are so directly tied to specific experiences and aromas.

Unlike home-cooked meals and happy or sad occasions, certain concepts are linked to fairly universal scent preferences. One such concept is that of cleanliness. Scents generally associated with cleanliness fall into three categories: fragrances of fruit or a fruit product—especially a citrus fruit—fragrances related to nature, especially those involving fresh air; and fragrances of cleaning products, such soaps, detergents, or shampoos.[13] Sometimes people associate a combination of one or more fragrance categories with cleanliness; for example, a particular brand of lemon detergent may be the scent they associate most with cleanliness. A similar pattern of answers emerges when people are asked about what they associate with uncleanliness; garbage, rubbish, and spoiled food lead the pack of responses.

This suggests a fundamental difference between the ways people associate scents with a concept such as cleanliness and a concept such as happiness. With a fundamentally emotional concept, such as happiness, the scent that is recalled is linked with a specific set of emotions derived from experiences connected with the idea. With a less emotional concept, such as cleanliness, the scent that is recalled is linked directly to the concept, so it is not based on a specific set of emotions or on a set of experiences. This means that the intermediate step of associating the scent with a specific experience, or memory, does not happen in the latter case, and this sidesteps the emotional connection.

When the emotional connection is absent, the cultural gap vanishes. That is why notions such as cleanliness or uncleanliness can be associated with fairly universal scent patterns. However, when the emotional connection is present, the cultural gap widens, and the fragrances to which notions such as happiness are linked differ from person to person and reflect each person's cultural heritage. This does not mean that people of a similar culture link the same scents with emotions such as happiness, but it does mean that the connections they do make will be more strongly influenced by their cultural background.

Although the cultural differences in odor preferences can sometimes be explained logically, they are also often seemingly arbitrary. For example, in the United States the smell of leather is perceived as conveying freshness or quality, but in Japan that smell is associated with dirtiness and animals. Advertisements for leather products sold in the United States tend to emphasize the leather odor, but in Japan such products are marketed with their scents eliminated or at least masked as much as possible. For marketers, it is essential to research culturally-based scent preferences before using a scent in developing a marketing campaign for a product (and even before developing the product itself).

SCENT MARKETING

Have you ever been in a new car and noticed the distinctive smell? Often known as "new car smell," this scent has become inextricably associated with new cars. If that scent is absent, people perceive the car to be of inferior quality and may even go so far as to buy chemicals to replicate the smell of the volatile organic compounds that usually produce this smell. In China, the smell is shunned, with people regularly attempting to eradicate the smell by drying tea leaves in their cars. In the United States, though, the smell is usually considered pleasant and desirable (but there is an element of personal preference to this as well).

The question is what to do with this knowledge in terms of marketing. Some steps are obvious: try to mask the smell in new cars sold in China and try to enhance that smell in cars sold in the United States. Indeed, the new car smell can be diffused in a dealership or a promotional booth to evoke the positive emotions associated with a new car before people even set foot into a vehicle. That scent can also be distributed directly through advertising. All of these efforts to bring the scent closer to the consumer take advantage of the connections between a scent and the emotions we expect consumers to associate with it.

Some clever ways to deliver scents to consumers are just now being pioneered. While there is not yet a way to convey scents over the Internet or television, there are scent strips that can be printed onto pieces of paper. Perfume makers have used these scent strips for years, but now marketers for products such as TV shows and politicians are adding scent marketing to their mix. The television show *Weeds* used such strips, namely, strips scented with marijuana, as part of magazine advertisements they ran. Their hope was that upon smelling the aroma of marijuana readers of the magazines would automatically connect the program to worry-free feelings of enjoyment and relaxation. A New York politician tried to use scent strips in a different manner by attaching them to mailings. When the mailings were delivered to houses and the scent strips were activated, they began to smell of garbage. One of the most universally disliked odors, the scent of garbage was supposed to invoke negative connotations that the recipient would then associate with the negative comments about the candidate's rival that were printed on the mailing. These types of advertising campaigns highlight the use of scent-based cues in evoking a particular emotion and linking that emotion to a product, person, or cause.

A different use of scent is in the form of ambient scents, which are present in the background of a setting without actively contributing to the main activities of the setting. Comparable to product scent, these types of scents are usually fainter and spread across an area rather than being associated with one specific product. Such scents, when perceived as pleasant, have been shown to increase spending when there was no music playing.[14] The effects vanished when music was introduced to the background as well, suggesting that providing too much stimulation, both auditory and olfactory, can actually negatively influence customer spending. Ambient scents can also decrease consumer perceptions of the passage of time.[15] This means that shoppers think they have been shopping for a shorter time when there is an ambient scent present as compared to when there is no ambient scent present. Note that the actual times spent shopping hardly changed; it was only the consumers' perceptions of time that varied significantly. These results also hold true for Internet shopping, but it is problematic for companies to manipulate the scents their customers will be exposed to if they are conducting their business over the Internet.

As with music, one important concept when dealing with ambient scents is that of congruence. The ambient scent must be perceived as not only pleasant but also congruent with the environment where it is found; otherwise, all positive effects of the ambient scent will be lost, and people who are exposed to the scent may even be led to feel awkward and out of place. While congruence is fairly easy to establish with music based on factors such as the age, gender, and ethnicity of the target demographic and the nature of the product being sold, it is not so easy with scents. To give an obvious example, there is no "elevator scent," and there is no "1970s scent," "rock scent," "pop scent," or "that scent that's always playing at clothing stores." There isn't even a radio or an iPod that can emit scents at will. While it can be painstaking to research and think about what scents would provide congruence given different types of stores, products, and locations, it is important to do so before considering whether to use an ambient scent because the benefits can so easily be lost when the scent is not congruent to the atmosphere around it.

Because scents are often linked so strongly to specific emotions, it can be easier to form links to brand names by using scent-based signatures than by using signatures that rely on other senses. Companies can use a certain scent that is not a primary attribute of their product, such as soap or shampoo, to differentiate their product from their competitors' products. If you had a positive experience with the scent of Ivory soap, for example, that experience, that scent, and the emotions that you feel in response to that scent would all become irrevocably linked to Ivory soap instead of just to soap in general. While the same phenomenon could occur if the soap had a particularly appealing shape or feel, the emotional connection of smell makes scent-based signatures the most conducive to brand recall and recognition.

A different example of a scent being attached to a product as a secondary attribute of the product is the scent that is infused into pens at Westin Hotels. The company adopted the strategy as a low-cost measure that could build brand recognition for the chain. Not only does the scent create a memorable experience for customers if they use the pen in the hotel room, but, if they take it with them and use it again, they are provided with a second exposure to the scent. That alone can be enough to remind them of their experience at the Westin, and, if it was positive, the scent of the pen could cause them to book with a Westin at a future date. Even if they are not exposed to the scent a second time, however, they are still more likely to be able to remember their stay at the hotel if they take in the scent once.

Another important idea in scent marketing is the concept of *adaptation*.[16] Much like with rod and cone adaptation that leads us to see better in dark rooms over time, adaptation of olfactory receptors leads us to eventually be able to ignore smells that we have been exposed to for a few minutes. This frequently happens in restaurants, where we are enticed by a smell only to order a dish and later find ourselves unable to smell the dish even though it is right in front of us. Interestingly enough, adaptation can be undone by removing exposure to the smell for as little as one minute. While restaurants provide a classic example of when adaptation comes into play, it also can happen with ambient scents or at perfume stores (or perfume departments). After spending some time in a perfume store, we are unable to distinguish as readily between perfumes, finding ourselves bogged down by the general combined scent of all the different types of perfume. In this type of cross-adaptation, exposure to a scent for an extended period of time causes us to lose sensitivity in distinguishing between similar scents. Such adaptations can heighten or lessen the benefits of a scent depending on the exact periods of time for which people are exposed to the scent.

One avenue of scent marketing some companies are exploring is downplaying scents that are associated with certain products rather than highlighting them. Trash bags, for example, are considered to be a disgusting product simply because of their association with garbage, which has a universally unpleasant smell. Various trash bag companies, such as Glad and Hefty, have laid claim to odor blocking technology that uses the properties of the chemicals in the garbage bag itself to mask the odor caused by its contents. By removing the associations of the garbage bag with the odor of garbage, the companies are attempting to remove many of the more emotional and memory-based negative connotations of garbage that are usually attached to the bags holding it. Some restaurants have a similar policy of controlling the scents of certain foods, such as fish, so that the aroma of their restaurant is not influenced by those scents but rather by the aromas of other foods, such as lemongrass. Starbucks even went so far as to stop serving hot breakfast items in some of its stores because the smells of those products was found to drown out the smell of coffee, which was what consumers expected to encounter in a coffee shop.

One avenue that some companies are taking is using smells to target people with certain cultural backgrounds. In an attempt to access the Hispanic market in the United States, Proctor & Gamble has worked to develop lavender-scented household cleaning products. The company believes that the scent of lavender is particularly appealing to Hispanics because it is more closely associated with their views of homely and womanly scents than some other, more traditional scents would be. Smaller stores catering primarily to one ethnicity, such as Asian grocery stores, benefit from the cultural differences in scent preferences unintentionally because the aromas of their products are more appealing to people of a certain descent than the aromas of a more mainstream establishment.

Some companies are even using smells in inventive (and sometimes silly) ways. A new line of aroma sticks claims to be able to facilitate weight loss when sniffed before eating meals (the efficacy of the sticks is not scientifically proven). There are now alarm clocks that can release scents as well as sounds to wake people up in the morning. More and more household products are going the way of the candle as aromatic options are explored and developed. While there is a fine line between usefulness, aesthetic pleasure, and silliness in incorporating scents into everyday products, there is no doubt that, on a large scale, scents as an element of marketing are here to stay.

CONCLUSION

We encounter and process a multitude of scents every day. Our olfactory system converts odor molecules into electric signals that we come to like or dislike over time. According to the learned view of scent preferences, most scent preferences are actually gradually acquired during the course of our lives rather than being innate. Many scents are linked directly to experiences and to the emotions we feel during those experiences; that is, the potential for connecting scents to emotions is greater than it is for any other sense. Similarly, regarding memory itself, I have shown that exposure to scents improves recall of attributes of a product even when the scent is not reintroduced when the attributes are being recalled.

The challenge marketers face is how to utilize the properties of scents effectively, both in terms of cost and in terms of efficiency. The development of scent strips has allowed some marketers to use the mail to distribute a scent to their target market. Others have opted to infuse scents directly into products or to introduce aromas into the functionality of what they design in order to access the emotional connections between scent and memory. The problem is felt most acutely by Internet and television marketers, where the technology to transmit scents does not yet exist and must be mimicked or suggested by using visual and auditory cues instead.

Transferring laboratory findings into products is neither an easy nor a quick process, and we are just now starting to see the development of products and marketing campaigns that are properly incorporating scents into their workings. As signature scents become more prevalent, the question of protection arises. Should it be possible to copyright or trademark a scent? From the perspective of marketers, answering in the affirmative certainly would seem to foster the growth of the scent marketing industry. If the answer is no, an entirely new level of complexity is introduced into the development of scents and their reengineering. Currently, only scents that are nonfunctional can be trademarked, and it is still not easy to get a scent trademark (though my research showing that product smell enhances product memory helps in obtaining one). Usually, such a trademark can only be obtained as part of a trademark for a greater signature that includes other elements such as the product's name or a visual representation of the product. This means that an orange juice company could not trademark the scent of oranges, but, if the same scent were adopted by an automobile or electronics company, that company might be able to prevent its competitors from copying that aroma.

So far, I have left the connections between smell and the other senses largely unexplored. This is because the sense of smell is most intricately connected with, that of taste, will be discussed in the next chapter. While it is not surprising to most people that smell and taste are connected, the degree to which they are linked often leaves people astounded. The majority of people have trouble telling apart what we would normally consider to be drastically different foods and beverages when deprived of their sense of smell. In fact, smell is just as important as taste when we determine the flavor of a food, and the science of understanding the sense of taste is incomplete without first having an understanding of the sense of smell.

Chapter 5

TASTE

TASTES OF THE WORLD

Think about your favorite restaurant. Now imagine your favorite dish from that restaurant. What is it that makes that particular meal so appealing? Many people would answer with something akin to "the taste of the food." But what exactly does taste mean in that context? Are they talking about the exact combination of sweetness, bitterness, saltiness, sourness, and the amount of umami that are in the dish? Probably not—they are using taste to refer to a combination of all of their senses that, in this case, is very pleasant. In all likelihood, the dish has an aroma and a look people find appealing. Even other factors, such as the price, the location of the restaurant, and the interior decor of the establishment, can make a difference. This would seem to suggest that taste as we know it is less of a sense by itself and more of an amalgamation of all our senses.

An example I use in my classes is asking students what they like about Hershey's Kisses. Is it the taste, the texture, the shape, the feel of the wrapping, or some combination of these? Of course, there is no right or wrong answer to this question; the results are interesting because they are so varied. Each person's answer will be slightly different even when referring to similar sensations. The sheer variety of different possible responses seems to suggest that there is more than just the taste of a food that makes it appealing. Clearly, Hershey's must have done something right in designing the Kiss to turn a simple piece of chocolate into a memorable cultural icon.

Going back to the restaurant example, many restaurants have begun to compete by appealing in interesting ways to several of our senses at the same time. For example, when Wendy's and Burger King launched their new versions of French fries, they emphasized not only that the new fries tasted different from the previous versions but also that they looked different. Arby's has already differentiated itself from other fast food restaurants by selling curly fries rather than fries with a more traditional shape. Kentucky Fried Chicken introduced extra crispy batter as an alternative to its original recipe to give its chicken more texture. Denny's sizzling entrees present an example of a product that emphasizes an auditory cue in the product's name.

The trend of marketing food products by emphasizing senses other than taste is growing particularly in high-end restaurants. In expensive restaurants and cooking schools, presentation is often valued just as highly as taste. The colors, textures, aromas, and even sounds of a meal are all considered to be of utmost importance. Seemingly trivial details, such as the shape of a pat of mashed potatoes or the design of a soup spoon, can subtly influence our perceptions of the entire meal. While Gordon Ramsay would have us believe that "However amazing a dish looks, it's always the taste that lingers," his assertion that one could eat with as much appetite from a pan as from a plate is obviously ludicrous. The combination and juxtaposition of colors and textures is not to be ignored either; usually, a dish is crafted in consideration of all of its sensory properties, and sometimes even an entire multiple course meal is designed to balance not only tastes but the attributes of our other senses as well.

Food products sold at grocery stores are not without cues appealing to senses other than taste either. When you choose a particular brand of food, what is your choice based on? Some people base their choice on their previous experience of the taste of a particular brand, and others might just choose the cheapest option. However, many people make their selection based on the design of the packaging or the visual properties of the product itself. Some people will even touch or feel the product, and still others might smell the product.

One explanation for these sorts of decision-making behaviors is that our other senses serve as substitutes for taste. Because we cannot usually taste a product at the supermarket before buying it, we use our other senses to assess its taste to the best of our ability. However, this is certainly not the case for food at restaurants, where we experience all the sensory properties of a plate of food almost simultaneously. Rather than considering the visual appeal of a dish as a substitute for taste, it is better to think of it as a component of taste. Taste is not so much a combination of receptors firing from our tongue as an amalgamation of all of our senses that combine with the information from those receptors on the tongue to form a perception of an object in our mouth.[1]

Considering taste as an amalgamation of the senses allows us to explain why food tastes better when it looks more appealing. It also helps explain why a dry cracker could taste better than a wet one, or why a cookie dipped in milk could taste better than the same cookie artificially flavored to imitate the taste of the milk. In the rest of this chapter, I will examine the scientific reasoning behind the theory of taste as an amalgamation of the senses and discuss several studies I have done that support this theory. I will also discuss its implications for marketing and provide examples of how companies are trying to stimulate your sense of taste with and without the help of changing the actual composition of the food they sell.

TASTE BUDS, THE TONGUE, AND THE BRAIN

Think back to grade school and try to remember the flavors you can taste and on what parts of your tongue the taste receptors for each of those flavors are located. Most likely, you can recall learning about the four tastes of sweetness, sourness, bitterness, and saltiness; saltiness and sweetness are located at the front of the tongue, bitterness is at the back, and sourness is on the sides (if you didn't remember, don't worry; it was a trap, and you would have been wrong anyway). While sweet, sour, bitter, and salty are four tastes for which we have receptors, there is actually a fifth taste, called umami (more on this later). In addition, the diagram of the tongue showing the taste buds in four regions is a complete myth.

In reality, there is no sweet or salty region of the tongue. The taste buds that detect the various tastes are located all across the tongue as well as in the back of your mouth and, strangely enough, in your intestine. The only exception is the very center of the tongue, which is comprised of a type of tissue that does not contain any taste buds. When taste buds are activated, they transmit their signals to the brain. The sense of taste appears to use specificity coding—that is, each neuron is wired to be activated by a stimulus of a specific quality. Thus, there are specific portions of the brain that are activated when presented with a particular type of taste or combination of tastes.

The other misconception is that there are only four tastes; in fact, there are five. The fifth taste is called umami, a word taken from the Japanese and meaning "pleasant savory taste"; it is perceived as meaty or brothy. The umami taste is activated by MSG, or monosodium glutamate, a spice most frequently used in Chinese cuisine. Contrary to popular belief, there is nothing dangerous or carcinogenic about MSG. In fact, the entire notion of "Chinese restaurant syndrome" as caused by MSG can be traced to a letter written to the *New England Journal of Medicine* in which a restaurant customer complained of feeling numbness after eating Chinese food. Recently, a California restaurant called Umami Burger has even tried to capitalize on awareness of the umami taste by creating products specifically appealing to it.

Unlike smell, taste is a sense whose responses are hardwired in the brain. This means that responses to many different tastes are programmed genetically rather than being learned or based on experience. Through experiments conducted on cloned mice, scientists were able to identify and remove certain genetic pathways that deal with the response to specific tastes. The cloned mice were unable to process a bitter taste, and in contrast to the original mice, they did not shy away from it.[2] Likewise, other mice were altered to have no affinity for sweeter tastes. Although not all humans dislike all bitter flavors, just as not all humans like all sweet flavors, the association of bitter taste with undesirable food and sweet with desirable ones is a hardwired response. Many bitter foods, such as grasses, are nutritionally inadequate, and sweeter foods with their higher sugar content are more desirable (nutritionally speaking). Though many people like some bitter foods, such as coffee, not many people would enjoy the taste of quinine.

While the hardwired response to tastes varies only minimally from one individual to the next, individual preferences for foods vary greatly among different people. Some of this variation can be attributed to the number of taste buds on a person's tongue. So-called supertasters have many more taste buds than the approximately ten thousand people usually have, and some people have considerably fewer. While a supertaster might find even a mild bitter taste repulsive, a person with fewer taste buds could find that same taste quite appealing. Some chemicals, such as PTC, or phenylthiocarbamide, can only be detected by a certain percentage of the population because many people lack the necessary number of taste buds to detect the taste of the chemical.[3] The detection of these chemicals is also connected to the relationship between smell and taste, which will be discussed in greater depth in the next section of this chapter.

TASTE AND SMELL

Here's a simple activity to illustrate the connection between taste and smell. Take out some small portions of various food items or beverages, and then taste a little bit of each, first while pinching your nose shut and later on with your nose open as usual. Do you notice the difference? Odds are you do, especially with certain foods or beverages whose aromas factor strongly into their flavor. If you want to, you can even have a friend set up a beverage lineup for you of different juices or types of soda. If you blindfold yourself and pinch your nose while tasting each drink, you'll probably have a lot of trouble identifying and distinguishing between the beverages. I'm not only talking about such similar products as Pepsi and Coke, but also about the differences between beverages such as Coke and Sprite or apple juice and grape juice.

Smell is such a crucial part of our ability to taste because odor vapors from the food we eat pass to the olfactory mucosa through a passageway at the back of our mouth. While pinching one's nose does not block that passageway, it prevents the circulation of air through the nose, which severely inhibits the flow of odor molecules from the mouth to the olfactory mucosa. The combination of the sensations of smell and taste in our brain then yields the flavor of a food. Blocking off the scent component of a flavor results in food tasting flavorless (or, at the very least, significantly different from what we would expect).

The absence or reduction of flavor when the sense of smell is obstructed during tasting has been documented in several laboratory studies. One such study had participants taste various chemicals while they were pinching their noses. While MSG was still perceived as salty, ferrous sulfate was perceived as tasteless rather than metallic, and sodium oleate was perceived as tasteless rather than soapy.[4] These results show that smell is involved in tasting chemicals we have never tasted before in their pure form and not only in processing the flavors of foods or beverages we have consumed before. Just because our ability to judge the flavor of a substance is impaired does not mean that we cannot gauge its other properties, such as its visual appearance (if not blindfolded) and its texture inside our mouths. This is why studies usually compare substances, such as different types of juices or drops of chemicals, that we would be unable to differentiate between without a correct assessment of their respective flavors.

Because flavors have both olfactory and taste-based components, it would make sense to expect that we like the taste of foods whose smell we like, and vice versa. This relationship usually holds true. Many of our favorite foods and our least favorite foods will have smells we find either very appealing or quite unappealing. There are a couple of products that serve as notable exceptions to this rule. Many people love the aroma of coffee or of a coffee shop, but they do not like its taste. The durian fruit, native to Southeast Asia, emits a powerful odor that many people liken to sewage or rotten onions. However, its taste is fruity, nothing at all like spoiled food. So many people dislike the aroma, and it is so strong and penetrating, that durian fruit has even been banned from many locations.

Research into the connection between smell and taste has led scientists to discover a second part of the brain devoted to taste. It is a part of the orbitofrontal cortex, or OFC, a region of the brain where the perceptions of tastes and smells are first combined. The OFC assists in processing experiences over and above the primary taste cortex, which receives input only from the sense of taste.

In addition to amalgamating smell into taste perception, the OFC also integrates responses from the other senses into what we perceive as taste. Not only is this the first location in the brain where smells and tastes are combined into flavors, it is also the first location where sights, sounds, and feelings are integrated with smells and tastes. When we perceive all of the different sensory components of a taste, our response is synergistic; that is, the combined flavor is more potent than the sum of its olfactory and taste-based parts. The psychology of taste is more complicated than simply dealing with a sensory response; other factors, such as the price of a product, how it has been described to us, its size, and our expectations of how it should taste, can influence our perceptions of its taste just as much as the actual sensory response does.

TASTE AS PSYCHOLOGY

In one of my experiments, I investigated whether the properties of a container can influence perceptions of the quality of the drink in it.[5] Using the same water, I had people rate the taste of water when it was consumed from a sturdy disposable cup and from a flimsy disposable cup. The water from the flimsy disposable cup was rated as significantly worse. All participants in this study drank the water through a straw so that the feel of the cup against their lips played no role. This suggests that the haptic (or touch-oriented) properties of the cup affect our perception of the liquid contained in the cup, and even when we are not conscious of those properties, they contribute to our perception of the liquid's taste. Note that this is not a haptic property of the water but only of the "package" containing the water. Similarly, researchers have found that a potato chip bag that is harder to open leads people to perceive the chips it contains as tasting better.[6]

The sense of touch can also impact our perceptions of foods when they are in our mouth. We feel the food in our mouth with our tongue as much as we taste it. Some properties of food, such as crunchiness, crispiness, dryness, softness, and wetness, are touch-based properties rather than strictly taste-based properties. Still, they contribute to our tasting experience and influence our perceptions of food. We might find a Nestlé Crunch bar that feels smooth unappealing, and we might find a Reese's Peanut Butter Cup that feels crunchy equally strange and repulsive. In this way, our expectations of the feel of a food in our mouth can influence how we perceive its taste.

Other touch-related properties of food factor into our tasting experience such as the temperature of the food. While most soups are served hot, gazpacho, a type of Spanish vegetable soup, is designed to be served cold. Eating gazpacho hot, or a bowl of chicken noodle soup cold, would be denying oneself part of the sensory experience of eating the product. The same phenomenon applies to beverages, and many people have strong preferences for hot or cold coffee and hot or iced tea. Temperature responses can also be evoked by certain substances; for example, menthol and spearmint produce a cooling sensation, and many spices, such as chili peppers, produce a sensation of heat. The word "hot" has become synonymous with "spicy" in American English because of this connection.

The connection between taste and hearing is often not as obvious because many foods do not as strongly appeal to our sense of hearing as they do to our senses of smell and sight. However, some product advertising, such as that for Nestlé's Crunch bar and Kellogg's Rice Krispies, tries to appeal to the connection between taste and sound. Some other foods now also have auditory signatures we associate with them. The melting of cheese on a pizza, the crunch of celery or of a carrot, and the sizzling sound of meat on a skillet are just a few examples of this. It turns out that these auditory components can strongly contribute to our tasting experience of the food associated with them.

One study examined this idea by having people eat potato chips while wearing headphones.[7] For some participants, the crunching sounds of the potato chip they were making were toned down, and for other people these sounds were amplified. People then rated the potato chips on properties such as freshness and crispness. The people who heard the amplified sound consistently rated the potato chips higher than those who heard only the softer sound. Interestingly enough, this is a phenomenon that is already being exploited by potato chip companies; most potato chips are specifically designed to be too big to fit into our mouths in one bite, and this is what causes us to make the distinctive crunching noise when eating the chips. Not only does this make other people around us want to consume potato chips, but it also influences our perception of the taste of the chips themselves.

I investigated the effects of the other senses on taste by exposing people to different catchphrases or descriptions of products and then having them rate the taste of the product.[8] The first such study I executed used two different taglines to describe a stick of gum: "Stimulate Your Senses" and "Long-Lasting Flavor." These taglines were actually used in the ads for two different brands of gum, 5 Gum and Extra. In the study, however, all of the participants were given identical sticks of gum. Participants who had been exposed to the tagline "Stimulate Your Senses" rated the gum as tasting significantly better than those who had been exposed to the other tagline. In addition, the multisensory tagline increased the number of positive sensory thoughts people had while chewing the gum.

I replicated the setup of the experiment with potato chips but used a longer description of the product that included either the two words "flavor" and "taste" or the two words "smell" and "texture." Once again, the multisensory description, using "smell" and "texture," led people to rate the taste of the potato chips as better and to have more positive sensory thoughts about the tasting experience. When I replicated the experiment a third time, this time using popcorn, I explored what would happen if people first had to accomplish a mental task. In that study, the multisensory description mentioned all of the five senses, but the other description mentioned only attributes of the sense of taste. The mental task involved memorizing several names. For those people who were subjected to the mental task, there was no longer any difference in the taste ratings following the two descriptions of the popcorn. This implies that when a person's mind is otherwise occupied, the ability to process information about a multisensory experience declines, and this can then influence taste perceptions.

A piece of unfavorable information, such as that the food was prepared in unclean conditions or that the food has passed its expiration date, can also influence our perceptions of taste. Not only are we disgusted by the unfavorable piece of information itself, but even in retrospect we believe the food itself to have tasted worse. Businesses certainly do not want to spread negative messages about themselves, but the rumor mill of the Internet creates plenty of unfavorable stories, including those found in competitors' advertisements. The fact that taste can be impacted retroactively has implications for the timing of advertisements, which can be just as effective in changing the opinions of people who have already tried a food product as in altering the views of potential new consumers. A positively received advertisement can cause us to believe in retrospect that a food product tasted better, much as a negative piece of information can affect our experience.

Events and life stages can impact our taste perceptions and preferences as well. Pregnant women often develop cravings for certain foods they did not like before their pregnancy. Sometimes, they also change their mind about foods they once liked. Such preferences can even be passed down to their children. Taste perceptions may also change over time; most of us disliked far more foods as children than we do in our adulthood, and, because we start to lose acuity in our senses of taste and smell as we age, certain foods can become either more or less appealing over time. On a smaller time scale, we have seasonal preferences for certain foods, such as for an ice-cold glass of lemonade on a hot summer day or a cup of hot chocolate to warm up on a frigid winter evening. In the next section, I will take a closer look at how our perception of properties such as size can influence our tasting experiences with regard to quality and quantity of food consumed.

SIZES, PORTIONS, AND CONSUMPTION

Suppose I presented someone with two bags of potato chips, one of which advertised claims that the chips are healthy, have no trans fats, are organic, and have other similar qualities. The other bag would not make those claims, but would be otherwise identical. Most people would report feeling better about eating the healthy chips than the unhealthy ones. This is fairly straightforward and consistent with the findings from the previous studies I described. It is important to note that people not only feel better about eating the healthy chips and that many also think those chips tasted better (or worse) because of their label, but they also are liable to eat more of the chips that are presented as healthy.

A number of other factors can change consumption of food products. Labeling wine as from the Sonoma Valley versus North Dakota causes consumption of the wine to increase.[9] Because California is known for its wine, and North Dakota is not, the California wine is perceived differently. The variety of products can also make a difference. When eating idly, people will consume almost twice as many M&M's when eating them from a bowl containing candy in ten colors versus compared to a bowl with candy in seven colors.[10] Likewise, a variety pack of yogurt with several flavors will be consumed more quickly than a pack of yogurt that is all of the same flavor. Even the layout of a package can matter; people will eat more from a box of items when the different shapes, colors, and types are organized in a random rather than a systematic order. This explains why all the caramels are in different corners of a chocolate box. While it may be annoying that you have to try and find your favorites, this also makes you eat more than if the chocolates were organized by flavor.

Figure 5.1 Chocolate Box Layout.
Some layouts of a chocolate box promote consumption, and others slow consumption. Generally, random ordering leads to a quicker finish for items such as boxes of chocolate. However, it's no fun when you're trying to find your favorite caramel or nougat.
Credit: © barneyboogles – Fotolia.com

Another factor that affects consumption is the size of the food product. By size, I mean not only the actual size in grams or ounces but also the perceived size, which is usually conveyed by some sort of qualitative label, such as "small" or "medium." When people buy a larger bucket of popcorn, they tend to eat more than when they buy a smaller bucket, even if the popcorn is stale.[11] The same holds true for drinks; people buying a 32-ounce soda from a fountain will drink more than if they buy a 20-ounce soda from the same fountain.

I tested the effect of labels on people's consumption by presenting them with a bag of mixed nuts and then asking them to estimate its weight.[12] When a bag with 60 pieces was labeled "medium," people estimated its weight at approximately 64 grams, but when the same bag was labeled "small," they estimated its weight at 51.78 grams. Surprisingly, this effect does not hold in reverse; when a 50-piece bag is labeled "medium" as opposed to "small," people think that its weight has increased only slightly.

I then extended the study to include consumption from the 60-piece bag of nuts. When the bag was labeled "small," average consumption was approximately 40 grams, but when it was labeled "medium," average consumption was approximately 30 grams. Perceived consumption, though, followed the opposite pattern, jumping from 46.3 grams to 53.9 grams when the bag's label was changed from "small" to "medium." Though people consumed less from the bag labeled "medium," they were under the impression that they had consumed more.

This phenomenon highlights a concept I have called *guiltless gluttony*: People generally jump at the opportunity to eat more without feeling bad about themselves, and there is no better chance to do so than when a package is labeled "small." Even when people do eat more, they still think that they have eaten less. Just as with the perceived size of the bag of nuts, though, this particular phenomenon doesn't work in reverse. When small sizes are labeled "large," people become skeptical, and their consumption patterns as well as their size perceptions are not significantly altered.

CRAFTING FOODS AND TASTES

What I have shown so far is that there is an art as well as a science to crafting the perfect taste. A taste is composed of more than just the stimulation of taste buds on the tongue. Many food companies and restaurants have realized this and have created packages and menus that appeal specifically to the psychological aspects of taste. One simple example of this is Starbucks. By emphasizing the coffee smell in its stores rather than the smell of a product, such as tea or pastries, the company has improved their customers' tasting experience. Starbucks has also renamed its cup sizes: short, tall, grande, and venti. Using such terms as "grande" and "venti" makes the coffee sound foreign, exotic, and more expensive than conventional size names would. The new names also confuse consumer expectations regarding product size, and thus customers find it harder to judge whether a venti drink is too small or has the correct size. In addition, the new size names distance Starbucks's coffee products from less expensive drinks such as sodas, which would use more conventional names.

The café Così uses a number of methods to improve the taste of its products. Many of its dishes are served with its distinctively shaped flatbread. The café's salads bear names such as "Adobo Lime Chicken" and "Wild Alaskan Salmon," which emphasize the uniqueness of the meats they contain. Even the serving dishes, such as salad bowls, have an unusual shape, being taller and narrower than one would expect. As you remember from the section on visual biases, we perceive containers of this shape as containing more than they actually do. All of these things, while seemingly aesthetic and quite purposeless, actually allow Così to differentiate itself from competitors such as Panera and to affect its customers' tasting experience.

Many restaurants with foreign cuisines have also been able to benefit from the multisensory aspect of taste. Distinctive fragrances and flavors, such as MSG with Chinese food, curry with Indian food, and the stew-like wat with Ethiopian food, help to set ethnic restaurants apart from more traditional establishments. Other factors, such as the decor and ambiance of the restaurant, can also contribute to an authentic, foreign feel, which in turn can influence our perception of the taste of the food. Some restaurants that rely especially on their aromas to enhance the flavor of their foods have even tried moving some of their cooking operations out of the kitchen to attract customers by exposing them to the scent of the food as it is being prepared.

In the opening section of this book, I mentioned the restaurant El Bulli in Spain. It has been a pioneer in the field of molecular gastronomy, a discipline that seeks to enhance the sensory experience of eating food by focusing on the chemical properties of foods. Many of the products served in that restaurant feature distinctive textures, shapes, temperatures, and chemical compositions. While some of the company's efforts are directly related to stimulating taste buds, others focus on touch-based aspects, such as the feel of the food in one's mouth. Many of those properties are the most difficult to duplicate; while it may be possible to replicate the chemical composition of a food, it can be very difficult to get the texture, the feel, and the creaminess just right. An easy example of this can be seen in preparing a soufflé. A professional chef will be able to prepare a much better tasting product than an amateur even if they both use the same ingredients. Likewise, the names of food products, if specific enough, can be protected by trademarks or copyrights, granting a degree of protection to part of the taste experience of those foods.

Supermarkets are no stranger to the multisensory nature of taste either. The quality of a product purchased from a clean, well-lit supermarket is more likely to be considered of a higher quality than that of one purchased in a market that looks dark or dirty. The visual appearance of food products at a supermarket not only affects their initial appeal to us but also our perception of those objects' taste. Many packaging designs, such as boxes, bottles, and cans, attempt to be visually appealing both to get people to buy the products and to enhance the perceived taste of the product. Most supermarkets periodically spray their fresh vegetables and fruits with water to ensure that they appear fresh. The spraying has no effect on the actual shelf life of the products; if anything, it actually causes them to spoil faster. However, from the perspective of the supermarket, being able to tap into the visual component that contributes to our notion of freshness outweighs the downside of increased spoilage.

One company that has used a quirky approach to tastes and flavors is Jelly Belly. Its jelly beans come in such exotic flavors as chocolate pudding, chili mango, and pomegranate. While these jelly beans are not quite at the level of Bertie Bott's Every Flavor Beans from the Harry Potter series, their lack of magical properties has not prevented the company from using descriptive words to enhance the experience of their taste. In addition, the company has partnered with soda companies such as Sunkist and A&W to craft flavors that its competitors cannot replicate. In theory, anyone can make a root beer or a cream soda jelly bean, but no company can make an "A&W Root Beer" or "A&W Cream Soda" jelly bean except Jelly Belly.

CONCLUSION

Taste is one of the most frequently misunderstood senses. Rather than being a sense unto itself, taste is better understood as an amalgamation of all our senses. Cues based on our senses of hearing, sight, touch, and especially scent can all affect our perceptions of taste. When people wear a blindfold and plug their nose, most are unable to distinguish between different types of juices or varieties of soda. When asked to identify flavors of energy drinks without looking at their color, people's average rate of correct responses is only around 20 percent. And when a drink is deliberately colored incorrectly, only just 40 percent of people can detect the error.[13] Visual and scent-based cues play such an integral role in taste that they sometimes take priority over cues from the taste buds in determining tastes.

From a marketing perspective, this means that companies dealing with food products can gain an advantage by appealing strongly to the other senses. As shown in my experiments with gum, potato chips, and popcorn, a multisensory tagline or advertising pitch actually increases the ratings of the products' taste. Many restaurants and food stores already do this, even if they do not fully realize what they are doing. Most meals are designed not just for superior taste but also for superior aroma and visual appeal. Many of the most expensive meals are distinguished from cheaper versions by differences in components of taste other than the ones provided by taste buds, namely temperature, name, and texture.

As scientists better understand tastes, they have become able to duplicate certain tastes with artificial chemicals. Many different types of artificial sweeteners already exist, and substitutes for salt that are considered healthier are not very far away. Replicating the other tastes (sourness, bitterness, and umami) can be accomplished by adding concentrated amounts of certain natural substances known to trigger those tastes. Thus, as these substitutes become more prevalent, it is not hard to imagine a world in which any given taste can be produced artificially. However, that scenario does not take into account the multisensory nature of taste, and anyone who thinks that artificial tastes will lead to food as we know it becoming obsolete is sorely mistaken.

The multisensory nature of taste can even help to bring us back to our roots. Eating has always been a social experience, from the Native American potlatch to the family dinner traditional in Western cultures. Maybe it is not such a bad thing after all that taste sensations cannot be copied; it would be strange to see a family united by Skype over the Christmas holidays and even more far-fetched to imagine them sharing an identical turkey taste strip programmed by Butterball or Honeysuckle. In an increasingly digitized world, the multisensory stimulus we perceive as taste will still be something we have to experience in person.

Chapter 6

TOUCH

THE ART OF TOUCH

It is well known that touch can be used to convey sympathy, as one might hug a friend who just lost a loved one, and that it can be used to show affection, as one might hold hands with one's sweetheart. But touch can do much more than that. Studies have shown that even while blindfolded people can identify another's emotion with remarkable accuracy based on a single touch lasting only a few seconds.[1] The notion of touch as powerful and able to convey more than just pressure is nothing new; in artworks, the Biblical scene of God imparting life to the body of Adam is usually represented as the two figures touching each other. In the field of medicine, touch is considered an important part of establishing a connection between a patient and a caregiver.

For marketers, who are neither art critics nor doctors, touch nevertheless takes on an equally great importance. The perception of touch, or haptics, is the only one that exists passively on all parts of our body. Unlike with vision, which is perceived through the eyes, or hearing, which is perceived through the ears, haptic sensations are not limited to any one specific location. We have haptic receptors on all parts of the outside of our body and even in some internal locations, such as in our mouths. This means that touch is not limited to haptic interactions with our hands—we can also touch a product with our mouths, toes, arms, or legs.

Touch allows us to perceive many properties of objects. Some of these primary attributes are hardness, texture, temperature, and weight. How we choose to touch an object depends upon which property we are trying to perceive. If you were trying to determine whether a pot is hot or not, how would you touch it? How about if you were trying to determine how much a small sphere weighs? Most people would touch the pot quickly so that if it is very hot, they will not get burned, and most people would hold the sphere in the palm of their hand and slowly raise and lower it.[2] These types of haptic interactions are specific to certain haptic properties; it would certainly be very strange if someone tried to figure out if a pan was hot by lifting it in the palm of their hand!

While hardness, texture, temperature, and weight are considered the primary haptic properties of objects because it is hard to determine any of those properties via the other senses, touch can also help us determine other attributes. Chief among these is shape. Usually, we would default to vision to identify the shape of an unknown object, but, when our sense of vision is impaired, our sense of touch takes over. For example, when people are in a dark room, they stumble around with their arms stretched out, attempting to pinpoint their location and avoid bumping into objects by using their sense of touch. One study investigated which attribute people would use to sort a group of objects of different shapes, sizes, degrees of rigidity, and texture.[3] When people were blindfolded, the primarily haptic properties, such as texture, dominated, but when people were allowed to look at the objects, the primarily visual properties, such as shape, were used more often as sorting criteria.

A different use of touch was introduced to the world by the Frenchman Louis Braille. As a child, Braille was educated at the school of Valentin Haüy, who had created volumes of manuscripts with raised lettering to teach the blind how to read. Not satisfied with that system, Braille developed a new system of writing consisting of a series of raised dots arranged in a two-by-three matrix. Different combinations and arrangements of raised dots represent the various letters of the alphabet. For the blind, this represented a revolutionary change in the way they could read, condensing the space necessary to print words and increasing their reading speed to almost a hundred words per minute. Today, Braille markings can be found in many public locations, including hotel room number placards and office building directories.

You can investigate how you might determine some of the haptic properties of objects by closing your eyes and having a friend bring you several objects from around your house or apartment (nothing that can be spilled and nothing from the trash, hopefully). Think about which properties you are trying to identify—are you trying to determine shape, texture, weight, temperature, or firmness? The answer is probably some combination of the five, though which properties you will perceive first depends, of course, on exactly which object you are trying to identify. Interestingly enough, most people can identify the majority of common household objects in just a few seconds using solely their sense of touch.[4]

Recently, marketers have begun to recognize the importance of using as many haptic properties in their products and advertisements as possible. Texture can be seen in the design of clothes, carpets, furniture, and even food (in our mouth). Weight can influence our perceptions of quality or calorie count, and so can hardness. As I explained previously, something as simple as drinking from a flimsy cup versus a sturdy cup can affect our perceptions of the drink we are consuming. More and more companies are playing up temperature-based aspects of their products, such as with toasted sandwiches and Icee slushed drinks.

In this chapter, I will take an in-depth look at different kinds of touch, differentiating between functional touch and touch primarily intended for aesthetic purposes. I will survey some of the research that has been done, and I will also explore how marketers are making use of those varieties of touch, highlighting several innovative products and advertising campaigns that have been developed recently. First, though, we must understand the science behind the sense of touch, in particular how we are able to perceive the haptic properties of objects marketers want to emphasize.

THE CUTANEOUS SYSTEM

Our fingertips are so sensitive that they can detect objects that are so miniscule that we cannot see them, such as spider webs. But why do we have such great sensitivity to touch? And how is it that certain areas of our body have so much more tactile acuity than others? The answers lie in the structure of our sense of touch. Our sense of touch, which is sometimes known as the somatosensory system, contains three main divisions. Two of these, proprioception and kinesthesis, deal with how we perceive our body and limbs in space and while they are in motion. Though

I will not discuss these systems at length because they are not as relevant from a marketing perspective, they do play an important part in our lives. For example, imagine waking up in the morning not knowing whether you're in your bed or floating on a cloud. The third system, which we will explore in more depth, is the cutaneous system. The cutaneous system deals with the perceptions of touch and pain originating from haptic receptors in our body.

Those haptic receptors, called mechanoreceptors, are primarily found in the upper layers of the skin. There are four main types of mechanoreceptors, and they are distinguished on the basis of two characteristics. Some mechanoreceptors fire only when a stimulus is perceived or stops being perceived. These receptors adapt fast and are different from receptors adapting more slowly that fire during the entire time a stimulus is present. Receptors also differ in the size of their field; while some receptors fire only when a stimulus is located in a very small patch of skin, others are wired to fire when a stimulus is presented anywhere in a greater area.

The characteristic of mechanoreceptors mentioned first is more useful in explaining how we are able to perceive haptic properties of objects such as their texture. While a slowly adapting receptor would fire continuously when in contact with a smooth surface, a fast-adapting receptor would fire only when the surface is encountered and then separated from the skin. If the surface was rough and abrasion occurred, the fast-adapting receptor would fire many times. The receptor adapting slowly, on the other hand, would fire continuously. Different receptor types also explain how we are able to perceive sensations such as vibrations. The size of a mechanoreceptor's field helps to explain why sensitivity varies in different areas of the body. Receptors in certain parts of the body have smaller fields, which makes them more sensitive, while receptors in other parts of the body have larger fields, which makes it harder for them to identify the exact location of a stimulus.[5]

When mechanoreceptors fire, they pass their signals first to the thalamus and then to the somatosensory cortex, the portion of the brain responsible for perceiving haptic signals. It is there that we are able to recognize what type of haptic signal has been relayed and from which part of the body it originates.

TYPES OF TOUCH

A dichotomy can be established between informational touch and hedonic touch.[6] Informational touch is used to gain information about an object. As exemplified in studies where subjects are asked to identify objects using only their sense of touch, informational touch accounts for the majority of our haptic experiences. Sometimes, informational touch can also be a means to an end that involves a different sense, such as when we hold a flower up to our nose to smell it. Hedonic touch involves haptic experiences we undergo simply for the sake of experiencing them. We might like the feel of soft velvet on our skin or enjoy the refreshment of ice cold water on our face after a workout.

In the jargon of academic marketing, informational and hedonic touch are related to the concepts of instrumental and autotelic touch. Instrumental touch refers to haptic exploration undertaken with the specific goal of making a purchase, such as feeling how soft a piece of clothing is or touching a piece of fruit to determine its ripeness. Autotelic touch refers to haptic exploration undergone for the sake of enjoyment, such as caressing your face with a feather.[7] In this way, instrumental and autotelic touch parallel the notions of informational and hedonic touch, but they are confined to the context of a retail environment.

One way to capture individual differences in haptic preferences is through a self-reported scale known as the *need for touch*, or NFT, scale.[8] Some people are naturally more inclined to value haptic experiences than others. There are also differences in the valuation of touch for the sake of aesthetics. The NFT scale thus has both instrumental and autotelic components. A typical component of the autotelic NFT scale is "Touching products can be fun," which people then rate based on how much that they agree with that statement; similarly, another component of the instrumental NFT scale is "The only way to make sure a product is worth buying is to actually touch it." How in tune are you with your sense of touch? Do you often find yourself touching people and products? My guess is that anyone who has taken the trouble to read this book will score high on the NFT scale.

Scoring higher on the NFT scale is neither a good thing nor a bad thing. Generally speaking, individuals with a higher NFT score will be more inclined to engage in autotelic or hedonic touching of objects, and they will derive greater pleasure from doing so. They may actually spend less time engaging in instrumental touching than individuals with a lower NFT score simply because the former are more efficient in using exploratory procedures to assess objects. When haptic cues contrast with or are presented in tandem with cues pertaining to the other senses, individuals with high NFT scores are more likely to place a higher value on the haptic cues. Just because you think you would score high or low on the NFT scale doesn't mean all of these trends hold true—keep in mind that these are only generalities across all people, not absolute laws for any given person.

TOUCHING A PRODUCT

Much of my research into the sense of touch has focused on its relation to the other senses. I wondered to what extent haptic properties could influence our perceptions of objects that were based on the other senses. Some basic examples of this phenomenon were provided in earlier chapters, such as the taste of a beverage being affected by the haptic properties of its container. For example, people will judge wine as tasting better when they have drunk it from a glass rather than from a plastic cup. Even a property such as the flimsiness or sturdiness of a cup can make a difference. What I wanted to explore is to what extent such relationships are actually driven by haptic interactions and whether different people would have different reactions to those interactions.

To investigate these questions, I returned to the setup of drinking water from a flimsy cup. I set up a study in which half the subjects felt the flimsiness of the cup when they drank the water and the other half did not. Furthermore, I divided the subjects into two groups—high autotelics (based on the NFT scale) and low autotelics. What I found was that interacting with the cup affected the taste of the water only for low autotelics.[9] For people in that group, interacting with the flimsy cup significantly lowered their judgment of the water's quality. For the high autotelics, interacting with the flimsy cup made virtually no difference in their judgment of the water's quality.

While this may seem counterintuitive at first glance, it actually makes a surprising amount of sense. High autotelics value the aesthetic nature of touch and generally enjoy the process of haptic exploration; thus, they are not fooled by what are essentially irrelevant haptic cues. They realize that informational touch regarding the cup is neither necessary nor appropriate in the context of determining the taste of mineral water. While high autotelics value haptic cues when these cues should determine their perceptions, they can also ignore those cues when they should not be relevant to their judgment. This is not the case for low autotelics, and their judgments of taste are more likely to be affected by haptic properties regardless of the scenario in which those judgments are being made.

I corroborated the results of this study by evaluating how much money high and low autotelics would be willing to pay for a bottle of sparkling mineral water. Half the participants were given a description of the product that included details of a flimsy bottle, and the other half received a description that elucidated the bottle's sturdiness. Again, for high autotelics the different descriptions of the bottle did not affect their evaluation, and both groups had similar numbers for their willingness to pay for the beverage. However, the low autotelics' willingness to pay was affected significantly ($1.72 compared to $1.57)[10]

What we've learned is that haptics can make a considerable difference from the perspective of a retailer—an extra
15 cents on a sale of just over a dollar and a half is quite
considerable.

A different avenue of exploration lies in the connections
between smell and haptics. If the haptic properties of an
object affect perceptions of taste, can they also influence
perceptions of smell? The problem with setting up a study
similar to the taste studies described above regarding taste
is that the nature of haptic interactions accompanying
smells are fundamentally different from those that accompany taste. While there is no doubt that the shape of a perfume bottle can influence perceptions of its fragrance and
can even be used as part of a sensory signature (remember
the iconic design of Jean-Paul Gauthier's perfume bottle
in the shape of a woman's torso), it would be a little silly
to investigate whether perceived smells of perfume are
affected by the flimsiness of the bottle.

In order to investigate a more concrete relationship
I looked at the connection between smell and haptics by
revisiting the notion of congruence. I theorized that certain
haptic properties could be linked to certain types of smell;
for example, would a feminine scent be associated with a
smoother surface? Would a masculine scent be associated
with a rougher surface? After fine-tuning two scents that
were perceived as equally masculine and feminine, I soaked
rough and smooth pieces of paper with both scents and
then asked subjects to evaluate the feel of the paper strips.
As expected, the rough paper was evaluated as better (feeling nicer and having a better texture) when scented with
the masculine fragrance, but the smooth paper was evaluated as better when scented with the feminine fragrance.[11]

Congruence between haptic properties and properties of the other senses has many implications. Sticking to perfumes, the congruence of the texture of the bottle and the targeted gender of the scent could impact consumers' perceptions of the efficacy of the product. Similarly with clothing products that are intended for females or males, incorporating roughness or smoothness into the product or the packaging can have a positive or negative impact on consumers' perceptions of the article of clothing based on whether the texture is congruent with the article's intended gender. In another study, I linked the scents of "pumpkin cinnamon" and "sea island cotton" to the concepts of warmth and coldness, respectively, and showed that gel packs that were supposed to heat or cool the skin were rated as more effective at doing so when their scents were congruent with their descriptions. I had the gel packs professionally wrapped with cloth and infused the cloth with the fragrances. Participants in the study felt that the gel pack was more effective at heating their hand when it was infused with the fragrance of cinnamon rather than that of sea island cotton. Conversely, people found that the gel pack was more effective at cooling their hand when it was infused with the smell of sea island cotton versus that of cinnamon. Even when the scent is not one that is by nature linked to a temperature-based haptic property, such as menthol to coldness, congruence is still important.[12]

Congruent haptic cues can also influence behavior in other ways. For example, when a feather or a piece of tree bark was included in a mailing for a charitable environmental organization, donations were shown to increase.[13] Forcing the recipient of the mailing to touch an object that has environmental connotations was enough to produce a more favorable opinion of the organization in the minds of some of the recipients. This is just one more example of how haptic interactions play an important role in our evaluation of sensory experiences.

THE POWER OF CONTAGION

If two packaged products touch each other, can their contact make any difference as to whether they are purchased? In fact, it can. The key to understanding why such incidental touch between products can affect the decision to buy them rests on the so-called *law of contagion*.[14] Dating back to the mystical and tribal beliefs of primitive peoples, the law implies that mere touch imparts some properties of each of the two touching objects to each other. For example, if a strawberry falls on a dirty floor, most of us would probably hesitate to eat it, even if it was then thoroughly washed or completely sanitized. The law of contagion helps to explain our behavior. In some sense, we cannot wholly dispense with the idea that some part of the essence of the filthy floor has been transferred to the strawberry. While the law of contagion is not entirely rational, it is also not entirely irrational, at least not from the perspective of our ancestors. Before we had the technology or the scientific acumen to clean that soiled strawberry and ensure that it was entirely clean, it probably wasn't a good idea for us to eat it.

The law of contagion has many implications for marketers. Certain products that elicit disgust, such as diapers, cat litter, or trash bags, should not come into physical contact with other products, especially food products.

Interestingly, the law of contagion only applies if the products are touching and not if they are merely near each other. It is as if only physical contact can transfer the unwanted properties from one product to the other. Even if contact with other products is brief, as far as consumers are concerned, the effects will not wear off easily or quickly once the products have been seen to touch. Studies have even shown that when consumers are forced to touch products they perceive as disgusting, they feel that they themselves are disgusting even after the contact has ended.[15]

Consumers may also observe other consumers touching a product. Interestingly, consumers are less likely to buy an item once it has been touched by another person. In most cases, the perceptions of such contacts are overwhelmingly negative. This presents a paradox of sorts; most people expect to touch certain products, such as fruit, blankets, and towels before buying them, and they even expect to try on clothes, but they are very put off by the thought of other consumers having touched those same products. Would you want to buy a shirt that you knew ten other people have tried on or eat an apple that ten other people have handled? Odds are the answer is no, even though you would wash the shirt or the apple before using either.

Again, the law of contagion is at work. But why does this happen? When we perceive consumers touching products, why does our opinion of those products automatically turn negative? Do we automatically think that the other person is disgusting? Given that we know nothing about the other person who touched the object, this makes no sense from a purely logical point of view. Our assumption should be that the other shopper was someone much like ourselves and thus, we hope, not too disgusting.

Some studies have removed that uncertainty by looking at what happens when we perceive men and women of varying degrees of cleanliness and attractiveness touching an object we wish to purchase. Somewhat surprisingly, the other person's cleanliness has little impact. Although an extremely unhygienic person may elicit even stronger feelings of disgust, even a perfectly clean person touching an object still causes us to perceive that object's value as lowered. The interaction is perceived as positive only when the other person is a very attractive member of the opposite gender. Even then, though, the effect is completely offset if a second, less attractive person interacted with the object as well. Of particular interest is the lack of support for the theory that popular objects, those that many people interact with, gain value from being touched repeatedly. If anything, it turns out that items many people have interacted with are perceived as especially disgusting.[16]

From the marketer's perspective, avoiding rejection by controlling which products are placed next to each other can be a difficult task, but is also an important one. This is why grocery retailers train baggers to pack chemical products, cat food, dog food, diapers, and cigarettes in separate bags from other food items.

CREATIVITY IN HAPTIC MARKETING

Recent advances in technology, coupled with marketers' increased awareness of the importance of emphasizing haptic properties, have led to an upsurge in the number of products and advertisements that utilize haptics in some way. Not only has the number of such products increased, but the degree to which haptics plays an important role has also gone up. In some cases, this has led to some zany and wild ideas, many of which have been wildly successful not only in gathering attention for products and building sensory signatures but also in boosting sales.

One of the craziest experiences that is catching on in the United States is the fish pedicure I discussed in the opening chapter. Imported from Asia, the idea of the fish pedicure provides a unique haptic sensation that is virtually impossible to duplicate. The feel of the fish combined with the water around them is strange and exotic. The experience allegedly also provides health benefits, as the fish are said to feed on dead skin from the feet, stimulating the growth of new skin and providing a feeling of rejuvenation. Even if the science behind the treatment is questionable, the haptic experience itself is what makes the fish pedicure so extraordinary.

Another example I discussed in the opening chapter is the iPod Touch. Here, the product's haptic property is emphasized by being incorporated into its name. The product then lives up to its name by interacting with the user via the sense of touch even though the primary output of the device, music, is auditory. By focusing on the haptic interaction in addition to the auditory component, Apple has added a new element to its product and its marketing campaign. By drawing consumers' attention to the interactivity of touch, Apple also made the human-product interaction much more personal and engaging. The distinctive advertisements for iPods, which used brightly colored backgrounds with people outlined in black and their iPods in white, coupled with the distinctive visual appearance of the iPod, highlight the product's multi-sensory signature. A similar strategy was adopted by the marketers of K-Y for the company's product TOUCH, a warming oil. K-Y focused on the haptic aspect of the product by simply naming it TOUCH. Although the lack of longer, more detailed sensory descriptors might seem to be counterproductive because customers may not know what the product does, the short and simple name highlights the haptic feeling, the main component of the sexual encounter. The name also carries an air of mystery, another quintessential ingredient of good sex. While K-Y struggled in the 1980s against competition from other over-the-counter products, it has reestablished itself as the primary brand name in its market due in no small part to its sensory-based campaign.

Other examples of suggesting a haptic property through a brand name are products whose name is based on or derived from the word "snuggle." The manufacturer of the fabric softener Snuggle claims that using its products makes clothing softer and will make everyone want to snuggle together. The Snuggie, a fleece overgarment that opens at the back and is designed for wearing around the house, also uses that association. By linking their product with the idea of snuggling, these companies evoke ideas of warmth and companionship, both of which their products claim to provide in some manner.

Other companies have incorporated haptic elements into their packaging. The Miller company used raised lettering in the design of the bottle for its Miller Genuine Draft beer so that consumers would feel the word "Miller" while drinking the beverage. Carlsberg has designed special bottles for sale at certain sports events, such as soccer games, that reflect elements of the game itself, such as raised soccer nets or soccer balls. While Orangina's bottle is known mainly for the visual design of its bottle, it serves as a haptic signature as well; the shape is as distinctive when handled as when it is seen. Some manufacturers of high-end sodas, such as Jones and IBC, use glass bottles rather than plastic ones to add weight and texture to the packaging of their drinks. This can heighten consumers' perceptions of taste and value

A different approach to packaging has been taken by the pharmaceutical company GlaxoSmithKline for its fat-blocking pill Alli. The pill is sold in a container designed to look and feel like a human hand, which can provide a sense of comfort and support for those struggling to lose weight. Combining both visual and haptic elements, the bottle not only acts as a distinctive sensory signature but also attempts to help people taking the pill with the psychological issues of losing weight. While the efficacy of the bottle in that latter regard is debatable, from a sensory standpoint its appeal is undeniable.

Many food companies use haptic properties either directly or indirectly. As I explained in the chapter on taste, several food products are associated with certain temperatures, such as hot and iced coffee or tea or hot and cold soups. However, other haptic properties are alluded to by different foods as well. Many caramels are manufactured in hard and soft varieties based on their firmness, and cookie companies such as Chips Ahoy make both chewy and crispy cookies that are baked for slightly different periods of time. The brand name of Tostinos, a company that makes frozen foods, such as pizza rolls, suggests the idea of "toast," which is associated with warmth, cooking food, and freshness. In Britain, potato chips are known as crisps, reflecting their haptic property of crispiness.

Some companies are going so far as to have their own labs set up dedicated specifically to addressing the sensory aspects of foods. Brands like Nabisco and Frito-Lay have realized that the cost of hiring specialists in the science of the senses is well worth the potential rewards. An innovative haptic property, even something as small as introducing a ridged potato chip or a cookie of a different shape or texture, could be worth millions of dollars when backed by the proper marketing campaign. Especially in industries where competition is intense, as is the case with packaged consumer goods, exploiting sensory properties can not only be a way to create fundamentally innovative products, it can also serve as a means for developing small ways to differentiate a particular product from the crowd of similar options on the market.

Haptic properties also play a role in video game controllers. The different designs of controllers for game systems, such as the Playstation, Xbox, Nintendo 64, Gamecube, and Wii, combine visual aspects and haptic properties. Some of the haptic properties are functional in that the controllers should facilitate ease of game play, but many serve primarily aesthetic purposes. Some controllers even are built to vibrate so as to simulate rough driving conditions or receiving blows in a fighting game. The Wii features a radically different two-part controller as well as add-ons, such as a steering wheel for racing games, and thus brings a whole new level of haptic interaction to the video game experience. The Kinect, Microsoft's add-on to the Xbox, has visual sensors, allowing players themselves to act as the controller.

As a final example that showcases a completely different aspect of haptics, I want to discuss the bus shelter marketing campaign for Kraft's brand StoveTop. The company installed advertisements in Chicago bus shelters that released heat in wintertime. This not only drew attention to the advertisement itself but it also tied in with the Stove Top product: meals that are made using the warmth of a stove. This meant that the heat in and of itself acted as a haptic tie to the warmth associated with the Stove Top product, thus creating congruence between the haptic cues. The campaign turned out to be very successful, garnering the attention of the media and boosting sales by 7 percent.

CONCLUSION

In this book, the last of the senses to be discussed is the sense of touch, or haptics, but it is certainly not the least important. Originating in the cutaneous part of the somatosensory system, haptic cues surround us every day. From the apple we touch at the grocery store to judge how ripe it is, to the candy bar we lift in our hand to determine its weight, to the piece of sandpaper we rub to assess its texture, our lives are filled with haptic interactions that are of interest to marketers. Increasingly, marketers have given us even more varied and exciting haptic experiences, such as heated advertisements, steering-wheel game controllers, and hand-shaped pill bottles.

One challenge facing haptic marketing is the lack of haptic interaction provided by the Internet. When we are touching only a mouse and a keyboard, it is impossible to have new or different haptic experiences, and certainly none so exotic as a fish pedicure. Even though touch is maintained in situations such as feeling the texture of the ground with a long stick or feeling the surface of a piece of paper with a pen, it is currently very difficult to replicate these scenarios using electronics in a glove or a bodysuit. The very number of haptic receptors in a hand that would need to be stimulated in perfect coordination in order to digitize even the simplest sensation of touch is astronomical. Technological innovations, such as bodysuits that can convey virtual realities of touch, are in the works, but it will be quite some time before any version of such technologies is available to the everyday consumer.

So far, I have neglected what is perhaps the most fulfilling type of touch—that of humans touching each other. One study showed that waitresses can make significantly more money in tips if they touch their customers or come into contact with them in some way, such as by sitting next to them in a booth.[17] This may be because touching another person causes an increase in the levels of oxytocin, a hormone generally associated with feelings of generosity. For marketers, human haptic interaction may have to take a backseat for the time being; however, it certainly plays a great role in our lives. After all, don't we all remember warm hugs from our parents? And how could we forget our first kiss?

We are just beginning to see many innovations in haptic marketing, and I anticipate that this trend will continue in the coming years. For every haptic sensation that has been used in marketing, there are many more that are yet to be developed and exploited. In the next chapter, I will look at some of the possible directions for sensory marketing in the future, both in terms of research from the perspective of the scientist and in terms of products from the perspective of marketers and consumers. I will also take a look at some sensory makeovers and wrap up by revisiting some of the most wonderful sensory experiences our world has to offer.

Chapter 7

CONCLUSION

CASINOS: A SENSORY EXPERIENCE

In the opening section of this book, I discussed the concept of sensory imagery, asking you to imagine a number of different scenarios to get a feel for how thoroughly you could imagine various scenarios involving your senses. Instead of being that specific to each sense, I'm now going to ask a more general question. Imagine a casino. What sensory attributes come to mind? What pictures do you see? What sounds do you hear? What aromas do you smell? What surfaces do you touch? What foods or drinks do you taste? It turns out that casinos are perfect examples of an environment that is carefully controlled to stimulate every one of your senses. The longer people play, the more money the house makes, so it's no wonder that casinos have worked very hard to perfect the sights, sounds, scents, tastes, and feelings their patrons encounter. The only mystery lies in discerning the specific effects of each cue.

Visually, casinos present a whirlwind of shapes and colors. Slot machines have gone from mechanical beasts to elegantly designed, brightly flashing electronic contraptions. Many of them feature columns and rows of lights, and their themes stand out in brilliant hues. Even card and craps tables are laid out very deliberately in a trademarked shade of green. Many casinos go to great lengths to establish signatures based on the themes of their artwork. The Bellagio's ceiling is home to the Fiori di Como, a sculpture of sorts executed in stained glass by Dale Chihuly. Caesars Palace plays on the idea of connecting to ancient times, featuring statues of Roman and Greek deities as well as staff members dressed in traditional costumes resembling senators, hoplites, and legionnaires. For their exteriors, as well, casinos go to great lengths to be appealing. On the Vegas strip, from the Luxor to the Mandalay Bay, every casino has a strong visual signature to set it apart from its competitors.

Casinos also have many auditory signatures. Perhaps the most obvious is the sound associated with a jackpot, which is akin to many coins clanging against one another or hitting a metal surface. Dating back to the times when machines actually paid out winnings in coins, the sound has become synonymous with winning. Hearing the noise actually fosters excitement and adds to the overall casino experience, making winning more enjoyable as well as making losing seem less frustrating. Even though actual coins do not come out of slot machines these days, the machines still makes the same noise. The only difference is that it is artificial. Many specific games have other noises associated with them. The sound of the ball as it whirls around the roulette wheel, bouncing from number to number, builds anticipation regarding where it will land. On card tables, the calls to the pit boss whenever a large sum of money is either taken in or paid out serve not only as a security measure but also as a way to reinforce in players the excitement of playing for high stakes. Even the sound of the cards leaving a shoe can be entrancing to players and become as integral to the game they are playing as the appearance of the cards.

Many people do not think of casinos as having an appealing smell. If anything, people tend to dislike the smell of casinos because most of them allow smoking. However, negative perceptions of scents in casinos are drastically reduced by air filtration units located throughout the establishments. While it is impossible to completely eliminate the odor of tobacco smoke, its impact can be mitigated through such extensive filtration systems. In restaurants, though, where it is important to maintain the aromas of food and not constantly supply fresh air, the level of circulation is decreased. When fresh air is pumped to the rest of the casino, many establishments choose to slightly raise the level of oxygen. Not only does this boost alertness so that people do not feel tired or fatigued, it also causes a feeling of exhilaration. While not technically a scent-based signature, this technique would never have been developed had it not been for casinos' desire to improve the aromatic quality of their air.

Taste is another sense that does not immediately come to mind for most people when thinking about casinos, but it is nevertheless manipulated by casinos, primarily in two ways. The first is by providing an excellent selection of restaurants in their venues. While this partially serves as a way to take advantage of winners who want to spend their profits, the restaurants also serve as an attraction for those not inclined to gamble. The second way in which taste is manipulated is by setting up free beverage stations and service throughout the casino. Most casinos do this because it provides an easy way to increase the satisfaction of patrons and does not force patrons to go outside the establishment for a drink or a meal. As with the pumping in of additional oxygen, the beverages, many of which contain sugar and caffeine, allow patrons to stay awake longer in the casino and become less likely to leave because they are tired or exhausted. Because the material cost of providing free beverages is so low, this is an effective way for casinos to keep the business of their patrons for as long as possible.

Casinos make use of haptics as well. Most of the games have a haptic component to them. While it would be easy for casinos to just have machines that work automatically, most require patrons to press several buttons to play. Some slot machines even have the handlebar that used to characterize older models so as to maintain the haptic experience some gamblers are used to. Gaming tables usually have a smooth, feltlike surface that serves as a texture-based signature. The most profound use of haptics, however, is found in casino chips. Instead of carrying around bills and trying to stuff them into their wallet or purse, players of table games use colored chips. This allows people to perform such actions as splitting their chips into two piles and then recombining them (as is commonly seen in poker games) and enables them to stack up ten chips for a bet rather than cumbersomely trying to stack ten five-dollar bills. In addition, the chips distort peoples' perceptions of value, causing them to place less value on a twenty-five- or one hundred-dollar chip than they would on five five-dollar bills or five twenty-dollar bills. This makes people more likely to bet, and thus more likely to lose, larger sums of money.

While many of the ways casinos appeal to the senses are obvious, that does not make them any less relevant from the marketer's perspective, nor does it make them any less potent as far as consumers are concerned. What is most interesting, or perhaps most scary, is that every signature that has been developed for casinos, and every technique they use, is entirely deliberate. If you go to a casino, keep in mind that every light, every shade of color, every sound, every aroma, every texture, and every taste is deliberately chosen. There is a reason that every sensory cue you perceive is there, and, more than likely, that reason does not bode well for whatever money you brought with you.

SENSORY MAKEOVERS: A PRACTICAL GUIDE

So far, I have discussed at length the different senses and how product attributes and advertisements appeal to them. However, I have largely neglected the process of how such properties were developed and thought of by marketers. While I have shown many different avenues of research that have shed light on the reasons why these properties are effective in marketing, I have not shown how businesspeople could go about using them. In what I term a *sensory makeover*, a product's advertising campaign, packaging, and message, and sometimes also the product itself, undergo significant changes to better take advantage of sensory marketing. Sensory makeovers can be quite drastic overhauls, or they can consist of a relatively minor alteration such as one major difference in either advertising, packaging, or product design in order to develop a sensory signature for the product. Major overhauls can include alterations in all of those aspects. It is important to keep in mind how much of a change needs to be implemented; too much can be just as harmful as too little, and creating multiple sensory cues can be confusing to consumers, especially when there is a lack of congruence. Accordingly, I will take a look at the types of changes that are most often implemented with respect to each sense.

One of the most recognizable types of a sensory signature is a logo. Designing a logo is a good way to create an image that consumers can then associate with a product. However, logos are really a dime a dozen these days, so crafting one that stands out from the crowd is just as important as crafting one that holds up to the competition. Once a product is already associated with a logo, switching logos can be risky, as is clear from the case of Gap when the company had to pull its new logo within two weeks of its debut. Pictorially,

Figure 7.1   Old and New Gap Logos.

Here are the old and new logos for the Gap. Unfortunately, the old logo became the new logo again after the other logo debuted to disastrous reviews. Sometimes, the potential consequences of a sensory makeover should be weighed before one embarks on that path.

logos can convey a theme or message by what they represent, such as the United States Postal Service's eagle, which symbolizes strength and speed. The colors chosen can also make a difference; red, white, and blue might be patriotic in the United States, but in another country the colors could easily have different meanings. Even a color itself can constitute a sensory signature, as in the example I discussed earlier of pink and the breast cancer movement. Another important visual aspect of a product that is sometimes overlooked is its packaging. The colors, letters, and pictures are important, and something as seemingly minor as the location of the product picture on the packaging can convey impressions of lightness (upper left) or weight (bottom right). Sometimes, packaging alone can be enough to craft a visual (as well as haptic) sensory signature, such as the perfume bottle of Jean-Paul Gauthier or the Orangina bottle. When making over the visual aspects of a product, it is paramount to remember that the visual components of advertisements and packaging will usually be seen before the consumer looks at the product, so even the most elegantly designed product may not be viewed as purchasable if it comes in an unappealing box.

The auditory equivalent of the logo is the slogan. Creating slogans that people will then link with products is an age-old marketing tactic. Having some sort of catchphrase that emphasizes key attributes of a product is a good way to get consumers to remember those properties. However, crafting the perfect slogan and then getting it to catch on with advertising can be quite expensive. A different approach comes in using the name of a product or brand itself to convey information about it. The advantage of this strategy is that it does not require the development of any other slogan or catchphrase, and consumers who know the name of such a product automatically have been exposed to the tactic as well. This is an approach to be used with caution, though, because changing a product's name can alienate customers, and it is much harder to institute a name change than to pull an ineffective slogan from a product. If a sound is already incorporated into the use of a given product, then that can provide the perfect window of opportunity for designing a sensory signature including that sound. A final approach to auditory branding is the jingle, a short song that is associated with a given product or brand. Jingles are another classic approach that has never fallen out of favor. While jingles can be expensive to develop and advertise, when they catch on, they can provide a level of connection and memorability for a brand that is hard to match. A different approach is to use a song as the background for an advertisement, keeping in mind the age of the targeted consumer group. Fidelity, an investment company, chose "Time of the Season," dating from 1967, to appeal to older listeners, while GM's advertisement during the 2012 Super Bowl featured "We Are Young," causing the song the jump to the top of the charts a couple of months later.

Using a scent as the basis of a sensory makeover can be very challenging. With vision and audition, a makeover in advertising or packaging can incorporate various aspects appealing to these senses; however, the sense of smell does not offer many such opportunities. Scent-based signatures are possible only for certain types of products; that is, they can be used properly only for products people will actually be able to smell, preferably before buying them. Moreover, the aroma used must somehow complement the product and be distinctive and memorable in its own right. Restaurants and food vendors present perfect examples of doing this; when restaurants have an appealing aroma, they can vent their kitchens directly onto the streets around the restaurant to attract walk-in traffic. Usually, though, aromas are used in conjunction with other aspects of a sensory makeover or as an auxiliary component of a product. For example, in the scented pens marketed by Westin, aroma is used in a small amount and in a noninvasive way as an effective method for boosting the memorability of an experience. A pleasant ambient scent can also be a good way to create a more positive atmosphere, especially if the experience of interacting with a product is emphasized in addition to consumers' experience of the product itself. For example, the DoubleTree Hotel has made a signature out of having fresh chocolate chip cookies ready for patrons when they check in, conveying a sense of warmth and comfort.

Taste is the most challenging sense to target simply because many products do not directly utilize it. Accordingly, I am in no way recommending that companies mail out taste strips to associate a certain flavor with a product that has nothing to do with taste. Nevertheless, taste-based marketing can be effective when used methodically and selectively. For food products, taste is obviously a major factor, so designing a taste, flavor, and texture consumers will find appealing can ensure that no part of the taste experience is left to chance. Some other products, such as mouthwash, vitamins, or cough syrup, are ingested through the mouth, so their taste can be an important part of the experience of consuming them. With such products, the idea of congruence comes into play once more; a coffee-flavored mouthwash, for example, might rank at the top in a taste test, but that does not mean that consumers will actually choose it in the store when it stands next to the mint-flavored mouthwash they have been using for years. Regarding the sense of taste, the most important thing to keep in mind is that taste is actually an amalgamation of all our senses and that working with taste involves keeping close tabs on a product's other sensory attributes.

Because haptic makeovers can deal with texture, shape, temperature, or rigidity, just to name the major properties, a plethora of permutations is available when deciding on what changes to make. Like vision, haptics is especially important to most products because it is guaranteed that they will be touched before they will be purchased (just as they are seen before being bought). Haptic makeovers are often paired with visual ones simply because the two senses go hand in hand where properties such as shape or texture are concerned. Haptic makeovers are most easily incorporated in the design of packaging. This is because haptics is exceptionally difficult to convey through advertising and because some products do not have strong haptic features associated with them. Even for a product such as a cold beverage, whose haptic properties are fairly fixed, it is possible to design a bottle, can, or jug that is very distinctive, not only in terms of shape or appearance but also in terms of sturdiness. Arizona, a brand of iced tea, built its packaging around tall, aluminum cans of tea as well as larger, plastic gallon-sized jugs when most companies use glass or plastic bottles. This allowed the company's product to be instantly identified in any convenience or grocery store and also gave Arizona's marketers more room to decorate the cans with themed pictures and patterns. For products that have haptic properties already incorporated into them, such as clothing or blankets, haptics is a great place to start developing appealing product design. For example, the most beautiful blanket will be picked up and then left on the shelf if it feels more like steel wool than velvet. Haptics can also be incorporated into the layout of a retail space. Gap displays jeans folded into a wall so that shoppers are forced to touch them. Seemingly mundane decisions, such as which products to put at the front of a store or on the front of a shelf, can also make a surprisingly big difference. In this way, utilizing the haptic properties of a product can go hand in hand with using the haptic properties of the environment in which that product will be sold.

Executing a sensory makeover is not an easy process. It takes proper planning and testing as well as proper execution. Don't be discouraged by failure; most products that are sensory successes today went through many less successful iterations. Designing a sensory marketing campaign and a sensory product is not a feat to be accomplished in a day. However, using the strategies outlined in this section is a good starting place for such an endeavor, which can ultimately prove to be very fruitful.

THE FUTURE OF SENSORY MARKETING

No overview of sensory marketing would be complete without taking a look at some of the latest directions of research. While sensory marketing has advanced very far as a field in the past ten years, it is still in its youth, and many scientists and academics are only just beginning to conduct experiments to answer the questions that have come to the forefront. One of the main areas of research is the interaction between the senses, where there are infinite possibilities for multisensory cues whose effects are not yet known. People seem to believe that "more is better," that products and places are better off the more sensory cues they emit—more smell, more color, more music, and so on. The notion of "more is better" is even taught in courses on sensory science; however, it is not always true. Too many cues can confuse people and overload them with information, or they can be synergistic, heightening the power of the cues' components. Sometimes, such cues are manipulated deliberately, but often they accumulate by accident due to the sheer number of sensory cues each of us processes all of the time.

There are also more specific problems and questions regarding each of the senses. Concerning vision, many researchers are focusing on imagery, trying to better understand the process of how we develop and process visual images. This is especially important in the context of advertising, where some advertisements with weaker visual components cause people to use imagery to envision the product described. Other researchers are trying to better understand the role of color. At the moment, there are only the two main connections between color and concepts (red and blue being connected to excitement and focus, respectively), but others may soon be discovered. The interplay between colors and shapes is also being investigated; in the same way as the color red and the octagon shape are processed as a stop sign, certain other combinations of colors and shapes represent concepts or ideas in our society.

While some of the findings regarding music are well understood, such as the effects of ambient music on shoppers and the connection between music preferences and age, there is also much that is yet to be discovered. The implications of multiple pieces of music being played in different parts of an advertisement or in different areas of a store are still unclear, but congruence is thought to play a major role in the effect. The notion of familiarity is also still unexplored. There may be connections between familiarity and pleasantness or between familiarity and perceived passage of time. Understanding this would help to better explain outcomes that are not accounted for by preferences in music alone. Other researchers are looking more closely at properties of voices, examining how speech rate and accent affect perceptions of the messages associated with a product.

In contrast to the mysterious aura surrounding smell's association with memory in the past nowadays much progress is being made in understanding our sense of smell. However, trends in individual scent preferences have yet to be studied. Currently, researchers are working on investigating differences in scent preferences based on gender, ethnic background, and age. Other research focuses on better understanding the effects of scents that are perceived below the threshold of awareness. If a person is not aware of perceiving a scent, does the fragrance still have a similar effect as when it is consciously perceived? For some aromas, this question is especially relevant because the human nose does not register their presence. However, since they are nevertheless present, it is possible that they could have a subconscious effect on our evaluations or memory of products and scent-based advertisements.

Taste is truly an amalgam of all five senses, which makes it difficult to identify directions of research in taste that do not involve the other senses as well. Identifying individual taste preferences, better understanding the role of advertisements and product messages in the taste experience, and testing the role of the environment in taste perceptions all require studying the other senses as well as taste. One interesting societal trend, fueled by the rise of dieting and healthy eating, is the stigma that has been placed on eating. In the Middle Ages, being corpulent was considered a sign of opulence and wealth because food was scarce for most people; nowadays, being overweight is often stigmatized as a character defect. Researching the effect on taste perceptions of product messages that reinforce or go against those trends would be one way to test how deeply engrained those social trends have become.

Many of the problems concerning touch are due to it often being used in very different ways by different subsets of consumers. Getting consumers to touch a product before buying it (or, conversely, getting them not to touch a product before buying it) can be quite a challenging task. By changing packaging design or altering the layout of store displays, retailers can seek to change the level of haptic interaction consumers have with products. However, the exact means of doing so, as well as the implications of such measures for individuals with a low or high need for touch, have not yet been explored. Other researchers have focused on trying to find substitutes for haptic interactions in scenarios where they are not possible, such as in the context of online shopping. Assessing the efficacy of haptically oriented descriptions is not an easy task, nor is crafting descriptions that can adequately replace haptic interactions (especially in the case of individuals with a high need for touch).

CLOSING WORDS

I often joke with my students that many people probably think that my vanity plate, which simply reads "sensory," is some sort of inappropriate reference. Not that I should care what people on the street think of me, but I would at least wish that readers of this book have a greater appreciation for my message. It is not merely that our senses provide us with many of our greatest pleasures in life; they form an integral part of what it means to be human. How we think about the world is directly influenced by how we see the world, how we hear the world, even by how we smell, taste, and touch the world. Perspective is defined by perception, and without perception, we would thus lose the perspective that makes us unique; we would lose both the point of view and the power of interpretation that make us individuals rather than automata.

Sensory experiences also constitute a fundamental component of our concept of leisure. In an increasingly mechanized society, our leisure activities have become more and more simplistic. Many people take vacations with the explicit purpose of doing as little as possible. But that's not what they really mean; what they're actually after is a purer sensory experience, free from the distortion and strife of everyday life. Lying on a beach, feeling the sand between one's toes as the warmth pulses through the softly yielding grains, is not an experience that would have been unfamiliar to the ancient Greeks or Romans. Yet, even after two thousand years, it is to such an experience that we so desperately seek to return—when we get the chance.

At the start of this book, I talked about two fundamentally different sensory experiences- that of the Ross faculty at the loss of their paper library and that of children who wonder in amazement at the new sensation of Dippin' Dots ice cream. Those experiences represent opposite manifestations of the recent push toward technological expansion. While the gains are myriad, as well as transparent and tangible, the losses are often more nebulous. It is difficult to say just what it is about being surrounded by volumes and volumes of books stacked to a ceiling twice one's height for as far as the eye can see that is so alluring. It is far easier to understand why one is enamored with the latest music release or enraptured by a new fragrance or perfume. In that way, maybe it is the sensory experiences that we are losing, rather than those that we are gaining, that don't often get their fair share of attention.

Either way, today's world provides a venue for exploring sensory experiences that is unprecedented in the course of human history. At no time have there been such great varieties of sensory experiences available for the average person to consume. And, as marketers become aware of this phenomenon, it is only logical that products themselves, as well as the advertisements endorsing them, will become more sensory in nature. Who knows, perhaps in fifty years the sensory experiences of advertisements will be just as powerful, potent, and enjoyable as the experience of the products they are trying to sell. Even amidst a sea of virtual realities and sensory advertisements, though, I would like to hope that there will still be the occasional paper library or store selling real ice cream. I, for one, think that it would be a shame if I couldn't enjoy my favorite novel lying on the beach, trying to eat a cone of mint chocolate chip ice cream before it melted under the fiery gaze of an afternoon sun.

NOTES

1 INTRODUCTION: WHAT IS SENSORY MARKETING?

1. Aradhna Krishna, "An Integrative Review of Sensory Marketing: Engaging the Senses to Affect Perception, Judgment and Behavior," *Journal of Consumer Psychology* (Forthcoming).
2. N. T. Tavassoli and Y. H. Lee, "The Differential Interaction of Auditory and Visual Advertising Elements with Chinese and English," *Journal of Marketing Research* 40, no. 4 (November 2003): 468–80.
3. Aradhna Krishna, "An Introduction to Sensory Marketing," in *Sensory Marketing* (New York: Routledge, 2010), 1–13.
4. George Berkeley, *Treatise Concerning the Principles of Human Knowledge* (Charleston, SC: Bibliobazaar, 2010).
5. C. W. Perky, "An Experimental Study of Imagination," *The American Journal of Psychology* 21, no. 3 (July 1910): 422–52.

2 VISION

1. Priya Ragubhir and Aradhna Krishna, "As the Crow Flies: Bias in Consumers' Map-Based Distance Judgments," *Journal of Consumer Research* 23, no. 1 (June 1996): 26–39.
2. Robert Krider, Priya Ragubhir, and Aradhna Krishna, "Pizza: Pi or Squared? The Effect of Perceived Area on Price Perceptions," *Marketing Science* 20, no.4 (2001): 405–25.
3. Brian Wansink and Koert von Ittersum, "Bottom's Up! The Influence of Elongation on Pouring and Consumption Volume," *Journal of Consumer Research* 30, no. 3 (December 2003): 455–63.

4. Priya Ragubhir and Aradhna Krishna, "Vital Dimensions: Antecedents and Consequences of Biases in Volume Perceptions," *Journal of Marketing Research* 36, no. 3 (August 1999): 313–26.

5. P. Valdez and J. Mehrabian, "Effect of Color on Emotions," *Journal of Experimental Psychology* 123, no. 4 (December 1994): 394–409.

6. J. R. Stroop, "Studies of Interaction in Serial Verbal Reactions," *Journal of Experimental Psychology* 18 (1935): 643–62.

7. X. Deng and B. E. Kahn, "Is Your Product on the Right Side? The "Location Effect" on Perceived Product Heaviness and Package Evaluation," *Journal of Marketing Research* 46, no. 6 (2009): 725–38.

8. See note 4.

9. Amitava Cattopadhay, Gerald Gorn, and Peter Darke, "Differences and Similarities in Hue Preferences Between Chinese and Caucasians," in *Sensory Marketing* (New York: Routledge, 2010), 219–40.

3 AUDITION

1. P. B. Denes, "On the Statistics of Spoken English," *Journal of the Acoustical Society of America* 35, no. 6 (1963): 892–904.

2. R. Hunt and T. Lin, "Accuracy of Judgments of Personal Attributes from Speech," *Journal of Personality and Social Psychology* 6, no. 4 (1) (August 1967): 450–53.

3. M. Zuckerman and K. Miyake, "The Attractive Voice: What Makes it So?" *Journal of Nonverbal Behavior* 17, no. 2 (1993): 119–35.

4. L. Oksenberg, L. Coleman, and C. F. Cannell, "Interviewers' Voices and Refusal Rates in Telephone Surveys," *The Public Opinion Quarterly* 50, no. 1 (Spring 1996): 97–111.

5. Darren Dahl, "Understanding the Role of Spokesperson Voice in Broadcast Advertising," in *Sensory Marketing* (New York: Routledge, 2010), 169–82.

6. N. Miller, G. Maruyama, R. J. Beaber, and K. Valone, "Speed of Speech and Persuasion," *Journal of Personality and Social Psychology* 34, no. 4 (October 1976): 615–24.

7. C. W. Park and S. M. Young, "Consumer Response to Television Commercials: The Impact of Involvement and Background Music on Brand Attitude Formation," *Journal of Marketing Research* 23, no. 1 (February 1986): 11–24.

8. R. E. Millaman, "Using Background Music to Affect the Behavior of Supermarket Shoppers," *Journal of Marketing* 46, no. 3 (Summer 1982): 86–91.

9. M. Holbrook and R. Schindler, "Some Exploratory Findings on the Development of Musical Tastes," *Journal of Consumer Research* 16, no. 1 (June 1989): 119–24.

10. E. Sapir, "A Study in Phonetic Symbolism," *Journal of Experimental Psychology* 12, no. 3 (June 1929): 225–39.

11. E. Yorkston and G. Menon, "A Sound Idea: Phonetic Effects of Brand Names on Consumer Judgments," *Journal of Consumer Research* 31, no. 1 (2004): 43–51.

4 SMELL

1. D. D. Laing, R. L. Doty, and W. Breipohl, *The Human Sense of Smell* (New York: Springer, 1991).

2. L. Buck and R. Axel, "A Novel Multigene Family May Encode Oderant Receptors: A Molecular Basis for Odor Recognition," *Cell* 65 (1991): 175–87.

3. R. S. Herz, S. L. Beland, and M. Hellerstein, "Changing Odor Hedonic Perception Through Emotional Associations in Humans," *International Journal of Comparative Psychology* 17 (2004): 315–39.

4. M. Stein, M. D. Ottenberg, and N. Roulet, "A Study of the Development of Olfactory Preferences," *Archives of Neurological Psychiatry* 80 (1958): 264–66.

5. E. A. Wasserman and R. R. Miller, "What's Elementary About Associative Learning?" *Annual Review of Psychology* 48 (1997): 573–607.

6. O. Robin, O. Alaoui-Ismaili, A. Dittmar, and E. Vernet-Mauri, "Emotional Responses Evoked by Dental Odors: An Evaluation from Autonomic Parameters," *Journal of Dental Research* 77 (1998): 1638–46.

7. R. S. Herz, "Ah, Sweet Skunk: Why We Like or Dislike What We Smell," *Cerebrum* 3, no. 4 (2001): 31-47.

8. G. Epple and R. S. Herz, "Ambient Odors Associated to Failure Influence Cognitive Performance in Children," *Developmental Psychology* 35 (1999): 103–7.

9. R. S. Herz, C. Schankler, and S. Beland, "Olfaction, Emotion, and Associative Learning: Effects on Motivated Behavior," *Motivation and Emotion* 28 (2004): 363–83.

10. R. S. Herz and J. von Clef, "The Influence of Verbal Labeling on the Perception of Odors: Evidence for Olfactory Illusions?" *Perception* 30 (2001): 381–91.

11. Aradhna Krishna, May Lwin, and Maureen Morrin, "Product Scent and Memory," *Journal of Consumer Research* 37 (June 2010): 57–67.

12. May Lwin and Mindawati Wijaya, "Do Scents Evoke the Same Feelings Across Cultures? Exploring the Role of Emotions," in *Sensory Marketing* (New York: Routledge, 2010), 109–22.

13. See note 12.

14. M. Morrin and J. C. Chebat, "Person-Place Congruency: The Interactive Effects of Shopper Style and Atmospherics on Consumer Expenditures" *Journal of Service Research* 8, no. 2 (2005): 181–91.

15. E. R Spangenberg, A. E. Crowley, and P. W. Henderson, "Improving the Store Environment: Do Olfactory Cues Affect Evaluations and Behaviors?" *Journal of Marketing* 60 (April 1996): 67–80.

16. J. D. Pierce Jr., C. J. Wysocki, E. V. Aronov, J. B. Webb, and R. M. Boden, "The Role of Perceptual and Structural Similarity in Cross-Adaptation," *Chemical Senses*, 21 (1996): 223–37.

5 TASTE

1. Aradhna Krishna and Ryan Elder, "The Gist of Gustation," in *Sensory Marketing* (New York: Routledge, 2010), 281–302.

2. K. L. Mueller, M. A. Hoon, I. Erlenbach, J. Chandrashekar, C. S. Zuker, and N. J. P. Ryba, "The Receptors and Coding Logic for Bitter Taste," *Nature* 434 (2005): 225–29.

3. H. Lawless, "A Comparison of Different Methods for Assessing Sensitivity to the Taste of Phenylthiocarbamide PTC," *Chemical Senses* 5 (1980): 247–56.

4. T. P. Hettinger, W. E. Myers, and M. E. Frank, "Role of Olfaction in Perception of Non-Traditional 'Taste' Stimuli," *Chemical Senses* 15 (1990): 755–60.

5. Aradhna Krishna and M. Morrin, "Does Touch Affect Taste? The Perceptual Transfer of Product Container Haptic Cues," *Journal of Consumer Research* 34 (April 2008): 807–18.

6. C. McDaniel and R. C. Baker, "Convenience Food Packaging and the Perception of Product Quality: What Does "Hard-to-Open"

Mean to Consumers?" *Journal of Marketing* 41 no. 4 (1977): 57–58.

7. M. Zampini and C. Spence, "The Role of Auditory Cues in Modulating the Perceived Crispiness and Staleness of Potato Chips," *Journal of Sensory Studies* 19, no. 5 (2004): 347–63.

8. Ryan Elder and Aradhna Krishna, "The Effect of Advertising Copy on Sensory Thoughts and Perceived Taste," *Journal of Consumer Research* 36, no. 5 (2010): 748–56.

9. Brian Wansink, Collin Payne, and Jill North, "Fine as North Dakota Wine: Sensory Expectations and the Intake of Companion Foods," *Physiology & Behavior* 90, no. 5 (April 2007): 712–16.

10. Barbara Kahn and Brian Wansink, "The Influence of Assortment Structure on Perceived Variety and Consumption Quantities," *Journal of Consumer Research* 30, no. 4 (March 2004): 519–33.

11. Nilufer Z. Aydinoglu and Aradhna Krishna, "Guiltless Gluttony: The Asymmetric Effect of Size Labels on Size Perception and Consumption," *Journal of Consumer Research* 37, no. 6 (April 2011): 1095–1112.

12. See note 11.

13. C. N. DuBose, A. V. Cardello, and O. Maller, "Effects of Colorants and Flavorants on Identification, Perceived Flavor Intensity, and Hedonic Quality of Fruit-Flavored Beverages and Cake," *Journal of Food Science* 45, no. 5 (1980): 1393–99.

6 TOUCH

1. M. Hertenstein, D. Keltner, B. App, B. Bulleit, and A. Jaskolka, "Touch Communicates Distinct Emotions," *Emotion* 6, no. 3 (2006): 528–33.

2. R. L. Klatsky and S. J. Lederman, "Stages of Manual Exploration in Haptic Object Identification," *Perception and Psychophysics* 52, no. 6 (1992): 661–70.

3. R. L. Klatsky, S. J. Lederman, and C. Reed, "There's More to Touch than Meets the Eye: The Salience of Object Attributes for Haptics With and Without Vision," *Journal of Experimental Psychology: General* 116 (1987): 356–69.

4. R. L. Klatsky, S. J. Lederman, and V. Metzger, "Identifying Objects by Touch: An 'Expert System,'" *Perception and Psychophysics* 37 (1985): 299–302.

5. A. B. Vallbo and R. S. Johansson, "The Tactile Sensory Innervation of the Glabrous Skin of the Human Hand," in *Active Touch* (New York: Oxford University Press, 1978), 29–54.

6. Roberta Klatsky, "Touch: A Gentle Tutorial with Implications for Marketing," in *Sensory Marketing* (New York: Routledge, 2010), 33–47.

7. Joann Peck, "Does Touch Matter? Insights From Haptic Research in Marketing," in *Sensory Marketing* (New York: Routledge, 2010), 17–31.

8. J. Peck and T. L. Childers, "Individual Differences in Haptic Information Processing: The 'Need for Touch' Scale," *Journal of Consumer Research* 30, no. 3 (2003): 430–42.

9. Aradhna Krishna and Maureen Morrin, "Does Touch Affect Taste? The Perceptual Transfer of Product Container Haptic Cues," *Journal of Consumer Research* 34, no. 6 (April 2008): 807–18.

10. See note 9.

11. Aradhna Krishna, Ryan S. Elder, and Cindy Caldara, "Feminine to Smell but Masculine to Touch? Multisensory Congruence and its Effect on the Aesthetic Experience," *Journal of Consumer Psychology* 20, no. 4 (October 2010): 410–18.

12. See note 11.

13. J. Peck and J. Wiggins, "It Just Feels Good: Consumers' Affective Response to Touch and its Influence on Attitudes and Behavior," *Journal of Marketing* 70, no. 4 (2006): 56–69.

14. P. Rozin and C. Nemeroff, "The Laws of Sympathetic Magic: A Psychological Analysis of Similarity and Contagion," in *Cultural Psychology: Essays on Comparative Human Development* (New York: Cambridge University Press, 1990), 205–32.

15. A. C. Morales and G. J. Fitzsimmons, "Product Contagion: Changing Consumer Evaluations Through Physical Contact With 'Disgusting' Products." *Journal of Marketing Research* 44 (May 2007): 272–83.

16. J. J. Argo, D. W. Dahl, and A. C. Morales, "Consumer Contamination: How Consumers React to Products Touched by Others." *Journal of Marketing* 70 (April 2006): 81–94.

17. L. E. Williams and J. A. Bargh, "Experiencing Physical Warmth Promotes Interpersonal Warmth," *Science* 322 (2008): 606–07.

AUTHOR'S BIOGRAPHY

ARADHNA KRISHNA IS THE DWIGHT F. Benton Professor of Marketing at the Ross School of Business, University of Michigan. Dr. Krishna received her PhD from New York University in 1989, her MBA from the Indian Institute of Management, Ahmedabad, in 1984, and her BA in Economics from Delhi University in 1979. Besides the Ross School, she has also spent time at Columbia University, New York University, and the National University of Singapore.

She is considered the pioneer of the field of sensory marketing. She defines sensory marketing as "marketing that engages the consumers' senses and affects their behaviors." Her research explores ways in which a product's look, feel, taste, sound, and smell contribute to how it is perceived, and how people respond to it. She has been working on sensory marketing since 1989 and has published several research papers on the topic. She organized the first sensory marketing conference, in Ann Arbor in June 2008, which was attended by academics from marketing and psychology and by practitioners. She has also edited a book on the topic, "Sensory Marketing: Research on the Sensuality of

Products," a compendium of academic research, released by Routledge in December 2009.

Besides the book, Prof. Krishna has also written an academic review paper on the subject, "An Integrative Review of Sensory Marketing: Engaging the Senses to Affect Perception, Judgment and Behavior," published in the *Journal of Consumer Psychology*. In addition to holding conferences and writing books and articles on sensory marketing, she has a research laboratory (sensorymarketinglab.com) where many of the ideas presented in this book have evolved.

Prof. Krishna is among the fifty most productive researchers in marketing having published more than sixty articles in the most prestigious outlets including the *Journal of Marketing Research, Marketing Science, Journal of Consumer Research, Journal of Consumer Psychology, Journal of Marketing, Harvard Business Review*. Her work has been cited in various periodicals such as *New York Times, Chicago Tribune, Huffington Post, LA Times, NPR, Economic Times India, Globe and Mail, Telegraph* (UK). She is lead Area Editor for the *Journal of Consumer Psychology*, area editor for *Management Science*, and serves on the editorial boards of *Journal of Marketing Research, Journal of Consumer Research*, and *Marketing Science*. She is also a fellow of the Society of Consumer Psychology.

She teaches sensory marketing to undergraduate business majors, MBAs, and executives across the world. She also consults with numerous firms on issues such as product design, package design, advertising and communication, and customer experience design. She has served on the Board of Directors of Northern Technology International Corporation, a consistent Forbes best 200 small company, consulted with several firms, and has also served as an expert witness.

She is a sensuist who enjoys drinking second flush Darjeeling tea in porcelain cups, collecting figurative art prints, listening to a-tonal jazz, cooking foods with strong aromas, and gardening without gloves.

ABOUT THIS BOOK

This book is a culmination of Dr. Krishna's attempts to develop the field of sensory marketing, or marketing that focuses on the five senses. From packaged goods to durables to service industries, sensory marketing is playing an increasingly important role in design and in advertising. Blending lessons learned from academic research and stories from the commercial world, this book is an invaluable asset for students and managers alike.

INDEX